Oxford **A-Z of Better Spelling**

D0168831

Oxford **A–Z of Better Spelling**

Second edition

Edited by
Charlotte Buxton

OXFORD
UNIVERSITY PRESS

OXFORD
UNIVERSITY PRESS

Great Clarendon Street, Oxford, OX2 6DP

Oxford University Press is a department of the University of Oxford.
It furthers the University's objective of excellence in research, scholarship,
and education by publishing worldwide. Oxford is a registered trade mark of
Oxford University Press in the UK and in certain other countries

© Oxford University Press 2004, 2007, 2009, 2013

Database right Oxford University Press (makers)

First published 2004
Reissued with new cover 2007
Second edition published 2009
Reissued with new cover 2013

British Library Cataloguing in Publication Data

Data available

Library of Congress Cataloging in Publication Data

Data available

ISBN 978-0-19-968462-5

Contents

Introduction

This new edition of the *Oxford A-Z of Better Spelling* provides a wealth of practical spelling help, focusing on the words which cause the most problems in daily life. If you want to create a good impression and get the right meaning across, correct spelling is vital, and the *Oxford A-Z of Better Spelling* is here to help. It's the perfect companion for anyone who wants to improve their spelling, whether at home, in the office, or at school or college.

This new edition has been revised and reorganized to make it even more helpful and easy to use. The in-text spelling rules have been updated and more new words have been added. Based on up-to-date evidence of the most common misspellings from our language databases, the *Oxford A-Z of Better Spelling* covers the established words which people often find difficult to spell (such as *accommodate* and *receive*) as well as tricky new entrants to the language (such as *karaoke* and *focaccia*).

Every entry has a short piece of spelling advice, written in a clear and straightforward way: there are rules on matters such as doubling letters when adding word endings, tips to help you remember spellings (such as **add** your **add**ress), and help on how to tell the difference between pairs of words which are often confused, such as *break* and *brake*. There are also useful links between words that begin with first letters which sound the same as other letters, so if you are not sure whether a word begins with *f*- or *ph*-, for example, and can't find it at *f*-, the link directs you to words beginning with *ph*-.

In addition to the main part of the book, there's a central reference section filled with information on spelling and grammar. This includes full and detailed explanations of spelling rules, guidance on the use of apostrophes and hyphens, and help with the spelling of beginnings and endings of words, such as whether you should write *–able* or *–ible* in words like *accessible*. There's also a section on American spelling, a table of common misspellings, and a discussion of how the spelling of words and phrases changes over time, and the methods we use to track those changes.

How to use this book

The *Oxford A-Z of Better Spelling* has been deigned to be clear and easy to use, with different types of information clearly marked, as shown below:

headword ·········· **charge** *noun and verb*

> **RULE:** Drop the final silent **-e** when adding **-ing** or **-ed**: charges, ·········· spelling rule
> charging, charged.

RELATED WORD: chargeable *adjective*

compliment *noun and verb*
! Do not confuse **compliment** with **complement**. See **COMPLEMENT**. ········ cross reference to another word or part of the book
RELATED WORD: complimentary *adjective*

conductor *noun*
Remember that the ending of ·············· spelling advice **conductor** is **-or**.
tip (called a ··········· **TIP:** a conductor directs an mnemonic) to help **or**chestra.
you remember a spelling

current *adjective and noun* ·············· part of speech
words that are ········ ! Do not confuse **current** with **currant**. often confused **current** means 'happening now' (*current events*) or 'a flow of water, air, or electricity' (*strong ocean currents*), whereas currant means 'a dried grape' (*currant cake*).
RELATED WORD: currency *noun*

Explanation of terms used in the book

accent
a mark that is put above or below a letter of a foreign word to show how a sound is pronounced or stressed, such as the mark (called an *acute accent*) over the e in the original French spelling of *café*.

adjective
a word that is used to describe a noun, such as *sweet*, *red*, or *technical*.

adverb
a word that is used to give more information about an adjective, verb, or other adverb, such as *very*, *really*, or *slowly*.

compound
a word made up of two or more existing words, such as *earring*, *left-handed*, or *credit card*.

conjunction
a word that is used to link other words or parts of sentences, such as *and* or *if*.

consonant
a letter of the alphabet that stands for a sound in which the breath is completely or partly blocked. These are *b*, *c*, *d*, *f*, *g*, *h*, *j*, *k*, *l*, *m*, *n*, *p*, *q*, *r*, *s*, *t*, *v*, *w*, *x*, *y*, and *z*.

infinitive
the basic, unchanged form of a verb, which usually occurs with the word 'to', as in *to go*, *to ask*, *to be*.

noun
a word that refers to a person, place, or thing, such as *book*, *Susan*, *England*, or *electricity*.

participle
the **past participle** is the form of a verb which is used to form certain past tenses (e.g. *looked* in *I have looked*) and sometimes as an adjective (e.g. *lost* in *lost property*). The **present participle** is the form of a verb, ending in -**ing**, which is used to form tenses describing something that is still happening (e.g. *I'm thinking*), nouns (e.g. *good thinking*), and adjectives (e.g. *running water*).

phrasal verb
a phrase consisting of a verb plus an adverb or a preposition which together have a particular meaning which is not deducible from the separate parts (e.g. *catch on*, *stick around*).

phrase
a group of words forming a unit within a sentence, such as *my friend Tim* in the sentence *I went to see my friend Tim*, or *two months ago* in the sentence *she left him two months ago*.

plural
the form of a noun that is used to refer to more than one person or thing, such as *books* or *churches*.

prefix
a letter or group of letters placed at the beginning of a word to change its meaning, such as **un-** (*unable*) or **pre-** (*predominant*).

preposition

a word that is used with a noun or pronoun to show place, time, or method, such as *on* in the sentence *put the bag on the chair*.

pronoun

a word that is used instead of a noun to indicate someone or something that has already been mentioned, such as *he*, *we*, or *they*.

stress

the emphasis that is given to a particular syllable or word in speech.

suffix

a letter or group of letters placed at the end of a word to change its meaning, such as -**able** (*breakable*) or -**ful** (*helpful*).

syllable

a unit of pronunciation that has one vowel sound and that forms all or part of a word. For example, the word *man* has one syllable, but *packet* has two (*pack* and *et*).

verb

a word that describes an action or state, such as *walk*, *be*, *do*, or *get*.

vowel

a letter of the alphabet that stands for a sound in which the mouth is open and the tongue is not touching the top of the mouth, the teeth, or the lips. These are *a*, *e*, *i*, *o*, and *u*.

abattoir *noun*
Spell **abattoir** with one **b** and a double **t**; the ending is **-oir** because it is a French word.

abbreviate *verb*
Remember that **abbreviate** and the related word **abbreviation** are spelled with a double **b**.

abdomen *noun*
The ending of **abdomen** is spelled **-men**, although the related word **abdominal** has an **i** after the **m**.

aberration *noun*
Remember that **aberration** has one **b** and a double **r**.

abet *verb*

> **RULE:** If a verb ends with a single vowel plus a consonant, and the stress is at the end of the word (as in *refer*), double the last letter when adding **-ing** or **-ed**: abets, abetting, abetted.

abhor *verb*
Spell **abhor** and the related word **abhorrent** with an **h** after the **b**.

> **RULE:** If a verb ends with a single vowel plus a consonant, and the stress is at the end of the word (as in *refer*), double the last letter when adding **-ing** or **-ed**: abhors, abhorring, abhorred.

-able
See centre pages for words ending in **-able** *and* **-ible**.

abscess *noun*
Remember that **abscess** is spelled with **-sc-** in the middle, and a double **s** at the end.

abseil *verb*
The ending of **abseil** is spelled **-seil**; it is a German word.

absorbent *adjective*
Remember that **absorbent** ends with **-ent**.

abysmal *adjective*
Spell **abysmal** with one **s**, but remember that the related word **abyss** has a double **s**.

accede *verb*
Remember that the ending of **accede** is **-cede**. *See centre pages for other verbs that end in* **-cede** *or* **-ceed**

accelerate *verb*
Spell **accelerate** and the related words **acceleration** and **accelerator** with a double **c** and one **l**.
TIP: I accelerated past the car, the cab, and the lorry.

accept *verb*
❗ Do not confuse **accept** with **except**. **Accept** means 'agree to receive or do something' (*she accepted the job eagerly*), whereas **except** means 'not including; apart from' (*I work every day except Sunday*).
RELATED WORD: acceptable *adjective*

access *verb and noun*
> Remember that **access** is spelled with a double **c** and a double **s**.
> **RELATED WORD:** accessible *adjective*

accessory *noun*
> Spell **accessory** with a double **c** and a double **s**; the ending is **-ory**.

> **RULE:** Make the plural of words that end in a consonant plus **-y** by changing the **-y** to **-ies** (as in *berry/berries*): accessories.

accommodate *verb*
> **Accommodate** should be spelled with a double **c** and a double **m**; remember that there is an **o** before and after the **m**'s.
> **RELATED WORD:** accommodation *noun*

accompany *verb*
> Spell **accompany** with a double **c** and one **m**.

> **RULE:** If a word ends in a consonant plus **-y** (as in *defy*), change the **-y** to an **-i** before adding any ending (unless the ending already begins with an **-i**): accompanies, accompanying, accompanied.

> **RELATED WORD:** accompaniment *noun*

accumulate *verb*
> Spell **accumulate** and the related word **accumulation** with a double **c** and one **m**.
> **TIP:** two **c**ups and a **m**ug had ac**c**u**m**ulated in the bowl.

achieve *verb* (achieves, achieving, achieved)

> **RULE:** **i** before **e** except after **c** (as in *thief*).

> **RELATED WORDS:** achievable *adjective*, achievement *noun*

acknowledgement *noun*
> **Acknowledgement** can also be spelled **acknowledgment**, without the **e** after the **g**: both are correct.

acquaint *verb*
> Remember that **acquaint** and the related word **acquaintance** are part of a set of words that begin with **acqu-**. Other words that are spelled **acqu-** include *acquiesce*, *acquire*, and *acquit*.

-acy
> *See centre pages for words ending in* **-acy** *and* **-asy**.

adaptor *noun*
> **Adaptor** can also be spelled **adapter**: both are correct.

address *noun and verb*
> Spell **address** with a double **d**.
> **TIP:** **add** your **add**ress.

admit *verb*

> **RULE:** If a verb ends with a single vowel plus a consonant, and the stress is at the end of the word (as in *refer*), double the last letter when adding **-ing** or **-ed**: admits, admitting, admitted.

> **RELATED WORD:** admittance *noun*

adolescent *noun and adjective*
> Spell **adolescent** with **-sc-** in the middle; the ending is **-ent**.

adverse *adjective*
> **!** Do not confuse **adverse** with **averse**. **Adverse** means 'harmful' or 'unfavourable' (*adverse publicity*), whereas **averse** means 'strongly disliking' or 'opposed' (*I am not averse to helping out*).

advertise *verb*
> Unlike most verbs ending in **-ise**, **advertise** cannot be spelled with an **-ize** ending. *See centre pages for other verbs that always end in* **-ise**.

RELATED WORD: advertisement *noun*

advise *verb*

Unlike most verbs ending in **-ise**, **advise** cannot be spelled with an **-ize** ending. *See centre pages for other verbs that always end in* **-ise**.
! Do not confuse **advise** with **advice**. **Advise** is a verb meaning 'suggest that someone should do something' (*I advised him to leave*), whereas **advice** is a noun that means 'suggestions about what someone should do' (*your doctor can give you advice on diet*).

adviser *noun*

Adviser can also be spelled **advisor**, although this is more common in American English. Remember that the related word **advisory** is always spelled with an **o**.

aerial *noun*

Aerial is one of a group of words based on Greek *aēr* 'air' and therefore spelled **aer-**. Other words that begin with **aer-** include *aerobic*, *aeroplane*, and *aerosol*.

aesthetic *adjective and noun*

Remember that **aesthetic** begins with **ae-**.
TIP: **a**rtistic **e**mbroidery has **ae**sthetic qualities.

affect *verb*

! Do not confuse **affect** with **effect**. **Affect** means 'make a difference to; change' (*the changes will affect everyone*), whereas **effect** means either 'a result' (*the drug has a painkilling effect*) or 'bring about a result' (*he effected a cost-cutting exercise*).

Afghan *noun and adjective*

Remember that **Afghan** has an **h** after the **g**.

aficionado *noun* (plural aficionados)

Spell **aficionado** with one **f** and **-cio-** in the middle; it is a Spanish word.

age *noun and verb* (ages, ageing or aging, aged)

Ageing is usually spelled with an **e**, although **aging** is also correct.

aggravate *verb*

Spell **aggravate** with a double **g**; there is an **a** before and after the **v**.
RELATED WORD: aggravation *noun*

aggression *noun*

Remember that **aggression** is spelled with a double **g** and a double **s**.
RELATED WORDS: aggressive *adjective*, aggressor *noun*

aggrieved *adjective*

Spell **aggrieved** with a double **g**.

RULE: **i** before **e** except after **c** (as in *thief*).

agoraphobia *noun*

The beginning of **agoraphobia** is spelled **agora-**; it comes from Greek *agora* 'public open space'.

albeit *conjunction*

RULE: When adding **all-** to words to make new words, **al-** should be spelled with only one **l**.

alcohol *noun*

Spell **alcohol** with **alco-** at the beginning.
TIP: drink **a** **l**arge **c**old **o**range juice, not **alco**hol.

align *verb*

Spell **align** with one **l**; the ending is **-ign**.

alkali *noun*

RULE: Make the plural in the usual way, by adding **s**: alkalis.

RELATED WORD: alkaline *adjective*

allege *verb*

Remember that **allege** has a double **l** and is spelled with **-ege** at the end.

alliteration *noun*

Spell **alliteration** and the related word **alliterative** with a double **l**.

allot *verb*

RULE: If a verb ends with a single vowel plus a consonant, and the stress is at the end of the word (as in *refer*), double the last letter when adding **-ing** or **-ed**: allots, allotting, allotted.

RELATED WORD: allotment *noun*

allowed

‼ Do not confuse **allowed** with **aloud**. **Allowed** means 'permitted' (*smoking is not allowed in the office*), whereas **aloud** means 'out loud' (*I read the letter aloud*).

all right *adjective and adverb*

Although **all right** can also be spelled **alright**, you should use **all right** in formal writing.

ally *noun and verb*

RULE: If a word ends in a consonant plus **-y** (as in *defy*), change the **-y** to an **-i** before adding any ending (unless the ending already begins with an **-i**): allies, allying, allied.

RELATED WORD: alliance *noun*

almighty *adjective*

RULE: When adding **all-** to words to make new words, **al-** should be spelled with only one **l**.

aloud *adjective*

‼ Do not confuse **aloud** with **allowed**. See **ALLOWED**.

already *adverb*

RULE: When adding **all-** to words to make new words, **al-** should be spelled with only one **l**.

alright

Do not use **alright** in formal writing. See **ALL RIGHT**.

Alsatian *noun*

Remember that the ending of **Alsatian** is spelled **-tian**.

altar *noun*

‼ Do not confuse **altar** with **alter**. An **altar** means 'a sacred table in a church' (*the high altar*), whereas **alter** means 'change something' (*she could not alter her fate*).

although *conjunction*

RULE: When adding **all-** to words to make new words, **al-** should be spelled with only one **l**.

altogether *adverb*

‼ Use **altogether** to mean 'completely' or 'on the whole' (*things were now altogether different*). Otherwise **all** and **together** should be treated as separate words (*the glue that holds them all together*).

aluminium *noun*

Remember that **aluminium** ends with **-ium** (the spelling **aluminum** is American).

always *adverb*

RULE: When adding **all-** to words to make new words, **al-** should be spelled with only one **l**.

amateur *noun*
Spell **amateur** (a French word) with -eur at the end.

ambassador *noun*
Spell **ambassador** with a double s; the ending is -or.

ambiguous *adjective*
Spell **ambiguous** with a u after the g, then -ous.

amend *verb*
Remember that **amend** and the related word **amendment** are spelled with a single m at the beginning.

amethyst *noun*
The ending of **amethyst** is spelled -yst.

amok *adverb*
Amok can also be spelled **amuck**; both are correct, although **amok** is far more common.

amount *noun and verb*
Remember that **amount** ends with -ount.

amphibian *noun*
The beginning of **amphibian** should be spelled **amphi-**; it comes from the Greek word *amphi-*, meaning 'both'.

amphitheatre *noun*
Spell **amphitheatre** with **amphi-** at the beginning; the ending is -tre (the spelling **amphitheater** is American).

anaemia *noun*
The beginning of **anaemia** and the related word **anaemic** should be spelled **anae-** (the spellings **anemia** and **anemic** are American).

anaesthetic *noun*
The beginning of **anaesthetic** and related words such as **anaesthetist** is spelled **anae-** (the spellings

anesthetic and **anesthetist** are American).

analogue *noun and adjective*
Spell **analogue** with -logue at the end (the spelling **analog** is American).

analyse *verb*
The ending of **analyse** should be spelled -yse (the spelling **analyze** is American). *See centre pages for other verbs that end in -yse.*

analysis *noun*

> **RULE:** Make the plural of **analysis** by changing the -is ending to -es: analyses.

-ance
See centre pages for words ending in -ance, -ancy, and -ant.

ancestor *noun*
Remember that the ending of **ancestor** is -or.
RELATED WORD: ancestry *noun*

anemone *noun*
Spell **anemone** with an n, then an m; it ends in -one.

annex *verb and noun*
The noun **annex** can also be spelled **annexe**: both are correct.

annihilate *verb*
Remember that **annihilate** and the related word **annihilation** are spelled with a double n, then -ih-.

anniversary *noun* (plural anniversaries)
Spell **anniversary** with a double n at the beginning; the ending is -ary.

announce *verb*
Spell **announce** and the related word **announcement** with a double n at the beginning.
TIP: the government announced nine new schemes.

annul *verb*

> **RULE:** Double the **l** when adding endings which begin with a vowel to words which end in a vowel plus **l** (as in *travel*): annuls, annulling, annulled.

> **RELATED WORD:** annulment *noun*

anonymous *adjective*
Remember that the middle of **anonymous** is spelled -**nym**-.

anorak *noun*
The ending of **anorak** should be spelled -**ak**.

answer *noun and verb*
Remember that **answer** has a **w** after the **s**, although it is not heard when you say the word.
TIP: she answered him slowly and wisely.

Antarctic *adjective and noun*
Remember that there are two **c**'s in **Antarctic**.
TIP: the Antarctic has a cold climate.

ante-
See centre pages for words beginning with **ante**- *and* **anti**-.

antecedent *noun and adjective*
Spell **antecedent** with -**ent** at the end.

antenatal *adjective*
Remember that **antenatal** begins with **ante**-.

anti-
See centre pages for words beginning with **anti**- *and* **ante**.

antidepressant *noun*
Remember that **antidepressant** is spelled with a double **s**; the ending is -**ant**.

antidote *noun*
Spell **antidote** with **anti**- at the beginning.

anxious *adjective*
Remember that **anxious** and the related word **anxiety** are spelled with an **x** after the **n**.

anyone *pronoun*
❗ Do not confuse **anyone** with **any one**, as the one-word spelling has a different meaning from the two-word one. Use **anyone** when you mean 'any person or people' (*anyone could do it*), but use **any one** to mean 'any single', as in *not more than twelve new members are admitted in any one year*.

apartment *noun*
Remember that there is only one **p** in **apartment**.

apologize, apologise *verb*
Spell **apologize** and the related word **apology** with -**olo**- in the middle.

apostrophe *noun*
See centre pages for information about using apostrophes.

appal *verb*
Spell **appal** with a double **p**.

> **RULE:** Double the **l** when adding endings which begin with a vowel to words which end in a vowel plus **l** (as in *travel*): appals, appalling, appalled.

apparatus *noun*
Remember that **apparatus** begins with **appar**-.

> **RULE:** Add -**es** to make the plural of words ending in -**s**: apparatuses.

apparent *adjective*
There is a double **p** in **apparent** but only one **r**; the ending is -**ent**.

appear *verb*
Spell **appear** and the related word **appearance** with a double **p**.

applaud *verb*
Spell **applaud** with a double **p**; the ending is **-aud**.
RELATED WORD: applause *noun*

apply *verb*

> **RULE:** If a word ends in a consonant plus **-y** (as in *defy*), change the **-y** to an **-i** before adding any ending (unless the ending already begins with an **-i**): applies, applying, applied.

RELATED WORD: appliance *noun*

appoint *verb*
Remember that **appoint** and the related word **appointment** are spelled with a double **p**.

appraise *verb*
! Do not confuse **appraise** with **apprise**. Appraise means 'assess something' (*I stepped back to appraise my handiwork*), while **apprise** means 'inform someone' (*I apprised him of what had happened*).
RELATED WORD: appraisal *noun*

appreciate *verb*
Spell **appreciate** and the related word **appreciation** with a double **p**.

approve *verb*
Remember that **approve** and the related word **approval** are spelled with a double **p**.

aquamarine *noun*
Spell **aquamarine** with **aq-** at the beginning: it comes from Latin *aqua* 'water', as do **aquarium** and **aquatic**.

aquarium *noun*
The plural of **aquarium** can be spelled either **aquaria** (as in the original Latin) or **aquariums**.

aqueduct *noun*
Remember that **aqueduct** begins with **aque-**.

-ar
See centre pages for words ending in -ar, -er, and -or.

archaeology *noun*
Spell **archaeology** with **ae** after the **h** (the spelling **archeology** is American).
RELATED WORD: archaeologist *noun*

archipelago *noun*
The plural of **archipelago** can be spelled either **archipelagos** or **archipelagoes**.

architect *noun*
Spell **architect** and the related word **architecture** with an **i** after the **h**.

Arctic *adjective and noun*
Remember that there are two **c**'s in **Arctic**.
TIP: the Ar**c**ti**c** has a **c**old **c**limate.

argument *noun*
There is no **e** after the **u** in **argument**, even though it comes from **argue**. It does not follow the usual rule that the final silent **e** is kept when adding endings that begin with a consonant.

armour *noun and verb*
Remember that **armour** and the related word **armoured** are spelled with **-our** (the spellings **armor** and **armored** are American).

artefact *noun*
Spell **artefact** with an **e** after the first **t** (the spelling **artifact** is American).

article *noun*
The ending of **article** is spelled **-cle**.
TIP: a **cle**ver newspaper arti**cle**.

a

-ary

See centre pages for words ending
with *-ary*, *-ery*, and *-ory*.

ascent *noun*

Remember that **ascent** and the
related words **ascend** and
ascendant begin with **asc-**.

! Do not confuse **ascent** with **assent**.
Ascent means 'the action of rising
or climbing up' (*the ascent of
Everest*), whereas **assent** means
'approval' or 'agreement' (*he
nodded his assent*).

asinine *adjective*

Spell **asinine** with a single **s** (it
comes from Latin *asinus* 'ass').

asphalt *noun*

Remember that the beginning of
asphalt is spelled **asph-**.

asphyxiate *verb*

Spell **asphyxiate** and the related
words **asphyxia** and **asphyxiation**
with **-phyx-** in the middle.

aspirin *noun*

Although it is pronounced *ass-prin*,
remember that **aspirin** should be
spelled with an **i** in the middle.

assailant *noun*

The ending of **assailant** is spelled
-ant.

assassinate *verb*

Spell **assassinate** and the related
word **assassination** with a double
s, then another double **s**.
TIP: **s**hoot, **s**tab, **s**trangle or
suffocate to a**ss**assinate.

assault *verb*

Remember that **assault** is spelled
with **-au-** in the middle.

assent *noun*

! Do not confuse **assent** with **ascent**.
See **ASCENT**.

assess *verb*

Spell **assess** and the related word
assessment with a double **s**, then
another double **s**.

assistant *noun*

The ending of **assistant** is **-ant**.

asterisk *noun*

The ending of **asterisk** should be
spelled **-isk**.

asthma *noun*

Remember that **asthma** is spelled
with **th** after the **s**, although it is
not heard when you say the word.

-asy

See centre pages for words ending in
-asy and *-acy*.

asymmetrical *adjective*

Remember that **asymmetrical** is
spelled with a single **s** and a double
m.

atheism *noun*

Spell **atheism** and the related word
atheist with **-ei-** after the **h**.

atrocity *noun* (plural **atrocities**)

Spell **atrocity** with a single **t** after
the **a**; the ending is **-city**.

attach *verb*

The ending of **attach** should be
spelled **-ach**. *See centre pages for
help with words ending in *-ach* or
-atch.*

attendance *noun*

Remember that **attendance** ends
with **-ance**.

attendant *noun*

Spell **attendant** with **-ant** at the
end.

attention *noun*

Remember that **attention** is
spelled with a double **t**; the ending
is **-tion**.

audience *noun*
Spell **audience** with **-ence** at the end.
TIP: en**tertain the audie**nce.

auditorium *noun*
The plural of **auditorium** can be spelled either **auditoria** (as in the original Latin) or **auditoriums**.

augur *verb*
❗ Do not confuse **augur** with **auger**. **Augur** means 'be a sign of a likely outcome' (*making any kind of profit augurs well for the future*), while an **auger** means 'a tool used for boring holes'.

aural *adjective*
❗ Do not confuse **aural** with **oral**. *See* **ORAL**.

autumn *noun*
Remember that **autumn** has an **n** after the **m**, although it is not heard when you say the word.
TIP: autum**n** has **m**any **n**ice aspects.

auxiliary *adjective and noun*
There is only one **l** in **auxiliary**.

available *adjective*
Remember that **available** ends with **-able**.

average *noun and verb*
Spell **average** with an **e** after the **v**; the ending is **-age**.

averse *adjective*
❗ Do not confuse **averse** with **adverse**. *See* **ADVERSE**.

avocado *noun* (plural avocados)
Spell **avocado** with an **o** after the **v**.

a

bachelor *noun*
Remember that the beginning of **bachelor** is spelled **bach-**.

bagel *noun*
The ending of **bagel** is spelled **-el**.

baguette *noun*
Baguette (a French word) is spelled with a **u** after the **g**; the ending is **-ette**.

baize *noun*
Remember that **baize** begins with **bai-**.

balloon *noun*
Remember that **balloon** is spelled with a double **l** and a double **o**.

ballot *verb and noun*

> **RULE:** Do not double the final consonant when adding endings which begin with a vowel to a word which ends in a vowel plus a consonant, if the stress is not at the end of the word (as in *target*): ballots, balloting, balloted.

balmy *adjective*
! Do not confuse **balmy** with **barmy**. **Balmy** is used about the weather to mean 'pleasantly warm' (*a balmy evening*), whereas **barmy** means 'stupid; crazy' (*a barmy idea*).

balti *noun*

> **RULE:** Make the plural of **balti** (an Urdu word) in the usual way, by adding **s**: baltis.

banister *noun*
Banister can also be spelled **bannister**, with a double **n**: both are correct.

banjo *noun*
The plural of **banjo** can be spelled either **banjos** or **banjoes**.

bankruptcy *noun*
Remember that the ending of **bankruptcy** is **-tcy**.

barbecue *noun and verb*
There is an **e** after the second **b** in **barbecue**; the ending is **-cue**.

> **RULE:** Drop the final silent **-e** when adding **-ing** or **-ed**: barbecues, barbecuing, barbecued.

bare *adjective and verb*
! Do not confuse **bare** with **bear**. *See* **BEAR**.

barmy *adjective*
! Do not confuse **barmy** with **balmy**. *See* **BALMY**.

barrel *noun*
Spell **barrel** with a double **r** and a single **l**.

basically *adverb*

> **RULE:** Add **-ally** (rather than **-ly**) when making adjectives that end in **-ic** (here, *basic*) into adverbs: **basically**.

basis *noun*

> **RULE:** Make the plural of **basis** by changing the **-is** ending to **-es**: bases.

bated *adjective*

❗ The phrase *with bated breath* (meaning 'in great suspense') should not be confused with **baited**, which means 'taunted' (*she teased and baited her brother*).

battalion *noun*

Spell **battalion** with a double **t** and a single **l**.

bayonet *noun and verb*

> **RULE:** Do not double the final consonant when adding endings which begin with a vowel to a word which ends in a vowel plus a consonant, if the stress is not at the end of the word (as in *target*): bayonets, bayoneting, bayoneted.

bazaar *noun*

❗ Do not confuse **bazaar** with **bizarre**. **Bazaar** means 'a market in the Middle East', whereas **bizarre** means 'strange' (*bizarre behaviour*).

bear *verb*

The different forms of this verb are: bears, bearing; the past tense is bore and the past participle is borne.

❗ Do not confuse **bear** with **bare**. **Bear** means 'carry' (*he was bearing a tray of food*) or 'put up with', whereas **bare** is an adjective that means 'naked' or a verb meaning 'uncover, reveal' (*he bared his chest*).

beautiful *adjective*

Remember that **beautiful** and the related words **beauty** and **beautify** are spelled with **beau-** at the beginning.

TIP: bare **e**legant **a**rms are **u**sually **beau**tiful.

because *conjunction*

Spell **because** with **-cau-** in the middle.

befit *verb*

> **RULE:** If a verb ends with a single vowel plus a consonant, and the stress is at the end of the word (as in *refer*), double the last letter when adding **-ing** or **-ed**: befits, befitting, befitted.

beggar *noun*

Spell **beggar** with a double **g**; the ending is **-ar**.

begin *verb*

> **RULE:** If a verb ends with a single vowel plus a consonant, and the stress is at the end of the word (as in *refer*), double the last letter when adding endings which begin with a vowel: begins, beginning; past tense began.

RELATED WORD: beginner *noun*

behaviour *noun*

Remember that the ending of **behaviour** is **-our** (the spelling **behavior** is American).

beige *noun*

Spell **beige** with **-ei-** after the **b**.
TIP: beige is **e**xtremely **i**mpractical.

beleaguered *adjective*

Remember that **beleaguered** is spelled with **-gue-** in the middle.

belief *noun*

> **RULE:** **Belief** and the related word **believe** follow the rule **i** before **e** except after **c** (as in *thief*).

RELATED WORD: believable *adjective*

b

belligerent *adjective*
Spell **belligerent** with a double **l**; the ending is **-ent**.

benefactor *noun*
The ending of **benefactor** is spelled **-or**.

beneficial *adjective*
Remember that **beneficial** begins with **bene-**.

benefit *verb and noun*

> **RULE:** Do not double the final consonant when adding endings which begin with a vowel to a word which ends in a vowel plus a consonant, if the stress is not at the end of the word (as in *target*): benefits, benefiting, benefited.

benevolent *adjective*
Spell **benevolent** with **bene-** at the beginning and **-ent** at the end.

benighted *adjective*
Remember that **benighted** is spelled **ben-** at the beginning (it is related to *night*, not *knight*).

benign *adjective*
The ending of **benign** is spelled **-ign**.

berry *noun*

> **RULE:** Make the plural of words that end in a consonant plus **-y** by changing the **-y** to **-ies**: berries.

berserk *adjective*
Remember that **berserk** begins with **ber-**.
TIP: Bertie went berserk.

berth *noun and verb*
! Do not confuse **berth** with **birth**. See **BIRTH**.

besiege *verb*

> **RULE:** **i** before **e** except after **c** (as in *thief*).

bhaji *noun* (plural **bhajis**)
Remember that **bhaji** (a Hindi word) starts with **bh-**.

bias *noun and verb* (**biases, biasing** or **biassing, biased** or **biassed**)
The verb forms **biasing** and **biased** are usually spelled with a single **s**, although the spellings **biassing** and **biassed** are also correct.

bicentennial *noun and adjective*
Remember that **bicentennial** has a double **n** before the ending.

biceps *noun*
The plural of **biceps** is the same as the singular: **biceps**.

bigot *noun*
Spell **bigot** with one **g** and one **t**.
RELATED WORD: bigoted *adjective*

billionaire *noun*
Remember that **billionaire** has a double **l** but only one **n**.
TIP: her lucky lotto numbers made her a billionaire.

binary *adjective*
Remember that **binary** ends with **-ary**.

binge *noun and verb*

> **RULE:** Keep the final **-e** when adding **-ing** to make sure that **bingeing** is pronounced with a soft -*ge*- sound: binges, bingeing, binged.

biriani *noun*
Biriani (an Urdu word) can also be spelled **biriyani** or **biryani**: all three are correct.

birth *noun*
! Do not confuse **birth** with **berth**. **Birth** means 'the emergence of a baby from the womb' (*he weighed six pounds at birth*), while **berth** means 'a place in a harbour for a ship,' or 'a bunk in a ship or other

means of transport' (*a four-berth caravan*).

biscuit *noun*
Remember that the ending of **biscuit** is **-cuit**.

bisect *verb*
Spell **bisect** with a single **s**.

bistro *noun*

> **RULE:** Make the plural of **bistro** in the usual way, by adding **-s**: bistros.

bizarre *adjective*
Remember that **bizarre** has one **z** and a double **r**.
! Do not confuse **bizarre** with **bazaar**. See **BAZAAR**.

blasé *adjective*
Blasé is usually spelled with an accent on the **e** (as in the original French).

blatant *adjective*
The ending of **blatant** is spelled **-ant**.

blizzard *noun*
Remember that **blizzard** has a double **z** in the middle.

blonde *adjective and noun*
Blonde can also be spelled **blond**, and both spellings can be used to describe men or women.

bluish *adjective*
Bluish can also be spelled **blueish**: both are correct, although **bluish** is far more common.

boisterous *adjective*
Remember that **boisterous** has an **e** before the **r**.

bonhomie *noun*
Bonhomie is spelled with an **h** after the **n**, although the **h** is not spoken because it is a French word.

bonus *noun*

> **RULE:** Add **-es** to make the plural of words which end in **-s**: bonuses.

bony *adjective*
Remember that the ending of **bony** is spelled **-ny**.

bookkeeping *noun*
Spell **bookkeeping** with a double **k**.

born *adjective*
! Do not confuse **born**, which means 'having started life' (*a newly born baby*) with **borne**, which is the past participle of the verb **bear** and means 'carried' (*the coffin was borne by eight soldiers*).

bough *noun*
! Do not confuse **bough** with **bow**. **Bough** means 'a branch of a tree' (*boughs laden with blossom*), whereas **bow** means 'bend the head' (*he bowed to his father*) or 'the front of a ship'.

boundary *noun* (plural boundaries)
The ending of **boundary** is spelled **-ary**.

bouquet *noun*
The ending of **bouquet** is **-quet**; the final **t** is not spoken because it is a French word.

bourgeois *adjective*
Remember that the ending of **bourgeois** is **-eois**; the final **s** is not spoken because it is a French word.
RELATED WORD: bourgeoisie *noun*

bow *verb*
! Do not confuse **bow** with **bough**. See **BOUGH**.

boycott *verb and noun*
Spell **boycott** with a double **t** (it comes from the name of Captain Charles *Boycott*).

Braille noun
Braille should be spelled with **-ille** at the end: the system is named after the French educationalist Louis *Braille*.

brake noun and verb
❗ Do not confuse **brake** with **break**. **Brake** means 'a device for slowing or stopping a vehicle' or 'slow or stop a vehicle' (*I had to brake hard*), whereas **break** mainly means 'separate into pieces' (*he managed to break a few ribs*) or 'a pause or interruption' (*a coffee break*).

brasserie noun
Spell **brasserie** with a double **s** and **-ie** at the end.

breach verb and noun
❗ Do not confuse **breach** with **breech**. **Breach** means 'break an agreement or rule' (*they breached the Data Protection Act*), 'break through something', or 'a gap', whereas **breech** means 'the back part of a gun barrel'.

break verb and noun
The different forms of the verb are: breaks, breaking; the past tense is broke and the past participle is broken.
❗ Do not confuse **break** with **brake**. *See* **BRAKE**.

breathalyse verb
Remember that the ending of **breathalyse** should be spelled **-yse** (the spelling **breathalyze** is American). *See centre pages for other verbs that end in* **-yse**.

breech noun
❗ Do not confuse **breech** with **breach**. *See* **BREACH**.

brief adjective and verb

> **RULE:** **i** before **e** except after **c** (as in *thief*).

brilliant adjective
Remember that **brilliant** has a double **l**; the ending is **-ant**.

brioche noun
Spell **brioche** with **-che** at the end; it is a French word.

broccoli noun
Remember that **broccoli** has a double **c** and one **l**; it is an Italian word.
TIP: bro**cc**oli is better than **c**abbage, **c**auliflower, or **l**eeks.

bruise noun and verb
Spell **bruise** with **-ui-** in the middle.

brunette noun
Remember that **brunette** has a single **n**; the ending is **-ette**.

bruschetta noun
Remember that **bruschetta** is spelled with **-sch-** in the middle; it is an Italian word.

brusque adjective
Spell **brusque** with **-que** at the end.

Buddhism noun
Remember that **Buddhism** and the related word **Buddhist** are spelled with a double **d** and then an **h** in the middle.

budget verb and noun

> **RULE:** Do not double the final consonant when adding endings which begin with a vowel to a word which ends in a vowel plus a consonant if the stress is not at the end of the word (as in *target*): budgets, budgeting, budgeted.

buffalo noun
The plural of **buffalo** is either the same as the singular or is made by adding **-es**: buffalo or buffaloes.

bulletin *noun*
Remember that **bulletin** has a double **l** but only one **t**.

bulrush *noun*
Bulrush can also be spelled **bullrush**, with a double **l**: both are correct.

bulwark *noun*
Remember that **bulwark** is spelled with a single **l**.

buoy *noun and verb*
Remember that **buoy** has a **u** before the **o**.
TIP: boats usually **o**pt to steer round a b**uo**y.
RELATED WORD: buoyant *adjective*

bureau *noun*
Spell **bureau** with -**eau** at the end; the plural can be spelled either **bureaus** or **bureaux** (as in the original French).

bureaucracy *noun*
Remember that **bureaucracy** and the related word **bureaucrat** are spelled with -**eau**- in the middle.

burglar *noun*
Spell **burglar** with -**lar** at the end.
RELATED WORD: burglary *noun*

burn *verb and noun*
The past tense of the verb **burn** can be either **burned** or **burnt**: both are correct.

burrito *noun* (plural burritos)
Remember that **burrito** has a double **r** but only one **t**; it is a Spanish word from Latin America.

bursar *noun*
Spell **bursar** with -**ar** at the end.

bus *noun and verb*

RULE: Add -**es** to make the plurals of nouns that end in -**s**: buses.

The different forms of the verb can be spelled with either a single or a double **s**: buses, busing, bused or busses, bussing, bussed.

business *noun*
Remember that **business** begins with **busi**-.

busy *adjective and verb* (busies, busying, busied)

RULE: If a word ends in a consonant plus -**y**, change the -**y** to an -**i** before adding any ending (unless the ending already begins with an -**i**): busier, busiest.

RELATED WORD: busily *adverb*

Cc

cactus *noun*
The plural of **cactus** can be spelled either **cactuses** or **cacti** (as in the original Latin).

cafe *noun*
Cafe is a French word, and can also be spelled **café**, with an accent on the **e**.

cafetière *noun*
Cafetière is a French word, and is usually spelled with an accent on the second **e**.

caffeine *noun*
Caffeine should be spelled with a double **f**, then **-ei-**; it does not follow the rule **i** before **e** except after **c**.

cagey *adjective*
Remember that the ending of **cagey** is spelled **-ey**.

calendar *noun*
Remember that **calendar** ends with **-ar**.
TIP: keep an **a**nnual **r**ecord on your calend**ar**.

calibre *noun*
The ending of **calibre** is spelled **-bre** (the spelling **caliber** is American).

calorie *noun*
Remember that the ending of **calorie** is **-ie**.

camouflage *noun and verb*
Spell **camouflage** with **ou** after the **m**.

campaign *noun and verb*
Remember that **campaign** ends with **-aign**.

canapé *noun*
Canapé is usually written with an accent on the **e** (as in the original French).

cancel *verb*

> **RULE:** Double the **l** when adding endings which begin with a vowel to words which end in a vowel plus **l** (as in *travel*): cancels, cancelling, cancelled.

RELATED WORD: cancellation *noun*

candour *noun*
The ending of **candour** is **-our** (the spelling **candor** is American).

canister *noun*
Remember that **canister** has only one **n**.

cannelloni *noun*
Remember that **cannelloni** has a double **n** and a double **l**; it is an Italian word.

cannibal *noun*
Spell **cannibal** with a double **n**, then an **i**.

canoe *noun and verb*

> **RULE:** Verbs ending in **-oe**, **-ee**, and **-ye** keep the final **-e** when adding **-ing**: canoes, canoeing, canoed.

RELATED WORD: canoeist *noun*

canvas *noun*
❗ Do not confuse **canvas** with **canvass**. Canvas means 'a type of strong cloth' (*a canvas bag*), whereas **canvass** means 'visit someone to seek their vote' (*party workers canvassed 2,000 voters*).

capellini *noun*
Spell **capellini** with a double **l**: it is an Italian word.

cappuccino *noun* (plural cappuccinos)
Spell **cappuccino** with a double **p** and a double **c**: it is an Italian word.

capsize *verb*
The ending of **capsize** is always spelled **-ize**. *See centre pages for help with verbs ending with -ize and -ise.*

carbohydrate *noun*
Remember that the beginning of **carbohydrate** is spelled **carbo-** and that it has **-hyd-** in the middle.

careful *adjective*
Remember that the ending of **careful** is spelled with a single **l**; it is made up of the word **care** plus the suffix (ending) **-ful**.
RELATED WORD: carefully *adverb*

caress *noun and verb*
Spell **caress** with one **r** and a double **s**.

cargo *noun*
The plural of **cargo** can be spelled **cargoes** or **cargos**, although **cargoes** is far more common.

Caribbean *adjective and noun*
Remember that **Caribbean** is spelled with one **r** and a double **b**.
TIP: the Caribbean has really beautiful beaches.

carnivorous *adjective*
Remember that the middle of **carnivorous** is spelled **-vor-**.

carriage *noun*

> **RULE:** If a word ends in a consonant plus **-y** (in this case, *carry*), change the **-y** to an **-i** before adding any ending (unless the ending already begins with an **-i**): **carriage**.

carrot *noun*
Remember that **carrot** is spelled with a double **r** but only one **t**.

cartilage *noun*
The ending of **cartilage** is spelled **-age**.

cartridge *noun*
Spell **cartridge** with the ending **-idge**.

cassette *noun*
Remember that **cassette** has a double **s** and a double **t**.

caster sugar *noun*
Caster can also be spelled **castor**: both are correct.

casual *adjective*
Spell **casual** and the related word **casualty** with **-ua-** after the **s**.

catalogue *noun and verb*
Remember that **catalogue** ends with **-logue** (the spelling **catalog** is American).

catalyse *verb*
Remember that the ending of **catalyse** should be spelled **-yse** (the spelling **catalyze** is American). *See centre pages for other verbs that end in -yse.*

catapult *noun and verb*
The ending of **catapult** is spelled **-pult**.

C

catarrh *noun*
Spell **catarrh** with a double **r** followed by a single **h**.

catastrophe *noun*
Remember that the end of **catastrophe** is spelled **-ophe**.
RELATED WORD: catastrophic *adjective*

caterpillar
The ending of **caterpillar** is spelled **-ar**.

cauliflower *noun*
Remember that **cauliflower** starts with **cauli-**.

caviar *noun*
Caviar can also be spelled **caviare**: both are correct.

-ceed
*See centre pages for verbs ending in **-ceed**, **-cede**, and **-sede**.*

ceiling *noun*

> **RULE: i** before **e** except after **c** (as in *receive*).

Celsius *noun*
Celsius should be spelled with a capital **C**, and with an **s** after the **l**: it is named after the Swedish scientist Anders *Celsius*.

cemetery *noun* (plural **cemeteries**)
Remember that **cemetery** ends with **-ery**.

censor *noun and verb*
! Do not confuse **censor** with **censure**. **Censor** means 'ban unacceptable parts of a book, film, etc.' (*it is impossible to censor the Internet*) while **censure** means 'criticize strongly' (*the country was censured for human rights abuses*).

census *noun* (plural **censuses**)
Remember that **census** ends with **-sus**.

centennial *adjective and noun*
Spell **centennial** with a double **n** and one **l**.

centimetre *noun*
The ending of **centimetre** is spelled **-re** (the spelling **centimeter** is American).

centre *noun and verb*
Remember that **centre** ends with **-re** (the spelling **center** is American).

> **RULE:** Drop the final silent **-e** when adding **-ing** or **-ed**: centres, centring, centred.

cereal *noun*
! Do not confuse **cereal** with **serial**. **Cereal** means 'a grass producing an edible grain, such as wheat', whereas **serial** means 'happening in a series' (*serial killings*).

certain *adjective*
Remember that **certain** ends with **-ain**.
TIP: she is cert**ain** to g**ain** a medal.

-ch
*See centre pages for words ending in **-ch** and **-tch**.*

challenge *noun and verb*
Spell **challenge** with a double **l**.

chameleon *noun*
Chameleon can also be spelled **chamaeleon**, with **ae** after the **m**, although **chameleon** is far more common.

chamois *noun*
Remember that **chamois** (a French word) ends with **-ois**; the spelling is very different from the way it is said.

chamomile *noun*
Chamomile can also be spelled **camomile**, without the **h**: both are correct.

champagne *noun*
The ending of **champagne** is spelled **-agne**.

chancellor *noun*
The ending of **chancellor** is **-or**.

changeable *adjective*

> **RULE:** Keep the final **-e** when adding **-able** to *change* to make sure that **changeable** is pronounced with a soft *-ge-* sound: changeable.

channel *noun and verb*

> **RULE:** Double the **l** when adding endings which begin with a vowel to words which end in a vowel plus **l** (as in *travel*): channels, channelling, channelled.

chapatti *noun*
Spell **chapatti** (a Hindi word) with one **p** and a double **t**.

Chardonnay *noun*
Spell **Chardonnay** with a double **n**.

charge *noun and verb*

> **RULE:** Drop the final silent **-e** when adding **-ing** or **-ed**: charges, charging, charged.

> **RELATED WORD:** chargeable *adjective*

chastise *verb*
Unlike most verbs ending in **-ise**, **chastise** cannot be spelled with an **-ize** ending. *See centre pages for other verbs that always end in -ise.*

chateau *noun*
The plural of **chateau** can be spelled either **chateaux** (as in the original French) or **chateaus**.

chauffeur *noun and verb*
Spell **chauffeur** with a double **f**; the ending is **-eur** because it is a French word.

cheetah *noun*
Remember that **cheetah** ends with **-ah**.

cheque *noun*
Spell **cheque** with **-que** at the end (the spelling **check** is American).

chestnut *noun*
Remember that **chestnut** is spelled with a **t** in the middle as well as at the end.

Chianti *noun*
Spell **Chianti** with a capital **C**, then **-hi-** at the beginning: it is an Italian word.

chief *noun and adjective*

> **RULE:** **i** before **e** except after **c** (as in *thief*).

chihuahua *noun*
Spell **chihuahua** with **-hua-** in the middle and **-hua** at the end; the dog is named after *Chihuahua* in Mexico.

chilli *noun*
Spell **chilli** with a double **l** (the spelling **chili** is American).

chlorine *noun*
The beginning of **chlorine** is spelled **ch-**.

chlorophyll *noun*
Remember that **chlorophyll** begins with **ch-**; the ending is **-phyll**.

cholesterol *noun*
Spell **cholesterol** with **ch-** at the beginning and **-sterol** at the end.

chord *noun*
❗ Do not confuse **chord** with **cord**. **Chord** means 'a group of musical notes' (*a G major chord*), whereas **cord** means 'thin string or rope' or 'a part of the body like a string or rope' (*the spinal cord*).

chorus *noun and verb* (choruses, chorusing, chorused)

> **RULE:** Add **-es** to make the plural of nouns that end in **-s**: *choruses*.

chrysalis *noun*
Spell **chrysalis** with a single **s** and a single **l**.

chrysanthemum *noun*
When you spell **chrysanthemum** think of the word bit by bit: the beginning is **chrys-**, the middle is **-anthe-**, and the ending is **-mum**.

ciabatta *noun*
Remember that **ciabatta** begins with **cia-**, followed by a single **b** and a double **t**; it is an Italian word.

cinnamon *noun*
Spell **cinnamon** with a double **n** in the middle; the ending is **-mon**.

circumcise *verb*
Unlike most verbs ending in **-ise**, **circumcise** cannot be spelled with an **-ize** ending. *See centre pages for other verbs that always end in **-ise***.
RELATED WORD: circumcision *noun*

circumference *noun*
Remember that the second part of **circumference** has three **e**'s in it: **-ference**.

cirrhosis *noun*
Spell **cirrhosis** with a double **r** followed by an **h**.

civilian *noun*
Spell **civilian** with a single **l**.

clamour *noun and verb*
Spell **clamour** with **-our** at the end (the spelling **clamor** is American).

claustrophobia *noun*
Spell **claustrophobia** with **claus-** at the beginning, followed by **-tro-**.

clearance *noun*
The ending of **clearance** is spelled **-ance**.

cliché *noun*
Cliché (a French word) is usually spelled with an accent on the **e**, although **cliche** is also correct.

climactic *adjective*
❗ Do not confuse **climactic** with **climatic**. Climactic means 'forming a climax' (*the film's climactic scene*), whereas **climatic** means 'relating to climate' (*global climatic changes*).

co- *prefix*
Some words which begin with **co-** are spelled with a hyphen, especially when **co-** is added to a word that begins with a vowel (such as *co-opt*). However, spellings without hyphens (such as *cooperate*) are becoming more common. *See centre pages for more information about hyphens.*

coarse *adjective*
❗ Do not confuse **coarse** with **course**. **Coarse** means 'rough' (*my hair is coarse and wavy*), whereas **course** means 'a direction' (*the plane changed course*).

cocoa *noun*
The ending of **cocoa** is spelled **-oa**.

coconut *noun*
Remember that the middle of **coconut** is spelled **-co-**.

coerce *verb*

> **RULE:** Drop the final silent **-e** when adding **-ing** or **-ed**: *coerces, coercing, coerced.*

RELATED WORD: coercion *noun*

coffee *noun*
Spell **coffee** with a double **f** and a double **e**.

coherent *adjective*
Spell **coherent** with -**ent** at the end.

coincidence *noun*
The ending of **coincidence** is -**ence**.

colander *noun*
Remember that **colander** begins with **col-**
TIP: **col**d pasta was left in the **col**ander.

collaborate *verb*
Spell **collaborate** with a double **l** and -**bor**- in the middle.

collapsible *adjective*
The ending of **collapsible** is spelled -**ible**.

colleague *noun*
Remember that **colleague** has a double **l** and ends with -**eague**.

collectable *adjective and noun*
Collectable can also be spelled **collectible**: **collectible** is usually used in the senses 'worth collecting' and 'an object valued by collectors', whereas **collectable** is usually used to mean 'able to be collected'.

collector *noun*
The ending of **collector** is spelled -**or**.

Colombian *adjective and noun*
Spell **Colombian** with an **o** in the middle as well as one at the beginning.

colonel *noun*
Remember that **colonel** begins with **colon-**; the spelling is very different from the way that it is said.

colonnade *noun*
Spell **colonnade** with a single **l** but a double **n**.

coloration *noun*
Coloration can also be spelled **colouration**: both are correct.

colossal *adjective*
Spell **colossal** with a single **l** then a double **s**.
TIP: large **s**aggy **s**horts made her look colo**ss**al.

colour *noun and verb*
Remember that **colour** ends with -**our** (the spelling **color** is American).

column *noun*
Spell **column** with -**mn** at the end.

combat *verb and noun*
The verb forms **combating** and **combated** are usually spelled with a single **t**, although the spellings **combatting** and **combatted** are also correct.

combustible *adjective*
Remember that the ending of **combustible** is spelled -**ible**.

commando *noun*

> **RULE:** The plural of **commando** is made in the usual way, by adding -**s**: commandos.

commemorate *verb*
Remember that **commemorate** and the related word **commemoration** are spelled with a double **m** then a single **m**.

commentary *noun* (plural commentaries)
Spell **commentary** with a double **m**; the ending is -**ary**.

commentator *noun*
The ending of **commentator** is spelled -**or**.

commiserate *verb*
Spell **commiserate** with a double **m** and a single **s**.

TIP: they commiserated in mutual misery and sadness.

commission *verb and noun*
Remember that **commission** has a double **m** and a double **s**.

commit *verb*

RULE: If a verb ends with a single vowel plus a consonant, and the stress is at the end of the word (as in *refer*), double the last letter when adding **-ing** or **-ed**: commits, committing, committed.

RELATED WORD: commitment *noun*

committee *noun*
Spell **committee** with a double **m**, a double **t**, and a double **e** at the end.

communicate *verb*
Spell **communicate** and the related word **communication** with a double **m**.

comparative *adjective*
Remember that **comparative** is spelled with **-ara-** in the middle.

compatible *adjective*
The ending of **compatible** is spelled **-ible**.

compel *verb*

RULE: Double the **l** when adding endings which begin with a vowel to words which end in a vowel plus **l** (as in *travel*): compels, compelling, compelled.

competent *adjective*
Spell **competent** with **-ent** at the end.

competitor *noun*
Remember that **competitor** ends with **-or**.

complacent *adjective*
❗ Do not confuse **complacent** with **complaisant**. **Complacent** means 'smug and self-satisfied' (*don't be complacent about security*), whereas **complaisant** means 'willing to please' (*the local people were complaisant and cordial*).

complement *noun and verb*
❗ Do not confuse **complement** with **compliment**. **Complement** means 'add to something in a way that improves it' (*the green sweater complemented her blonde hair*) or 'an addition that improves the original', whereas **compliment** means 'praise someone or something' (*he complimented her on her appearance*) or 'an admiring remark'.
RELATED WORD: complementary *adjective*

complexion *noun*
Spell **complexion** with an **x** in the middle.

complicit *adjective*
Remember that **complicit** and the related word **complicity** are spelled with a **c** before the second **i**.

compliment *noun and verb*
❗ Do not confuse **compliment** with **complement**. *See* **COMPLEMENT**.
RELATED WORD: complimentary *adjective*

component *noun*
Remember that **component** ends with **-ent**.

comprehensible *adjective*
Spell **comprehensible** with **-ible** at the end.

comprise *verb*
Unlike most verbs ending in **-ise**, **comprise** cannot be spelled with an **-ize** ending. *See centre pages for other verbs that always end in **-ise**.*

compromise *noun and verb*
Compromise cannot be spelled with an **-ize** ending. *See centre pages for other verbs that always end in -ise.*

compulsory *adjective*
The ending of **compulsory** is spelled **-ory**.

computer *noun*
Remember that **computer** ends with **-er**.

concede *verb*
Spell **concede** with **-cede** at the end. *See centre pages for other verbs that end in -cede or -ceed.*

conceit *noun*
RULE: **i** before **e** except after **c** (as in *receive*).

conceive *verb*
RULE: **i** before **e** except after **c** (as in *receive*).

conciliate *verb*
Remember that **conciliate** is spelled with a single **l**.
RELATED WORD: conciliation *noun*

concur *verb*
RULE: If a verb ends with a single vowel plus a consonant, and the stress is at the end of the word (as in *refer*), double the last letter when adding endings which begin with a vowel: concurs, concurring, concurred.

RELATED WORD: concurrent *adjective*

condemn *verb*
Remember that **condemn** ends with **-mn**.

condescend *verb*
Spell **condescend** with **-esc-** in the middle.

conductor *noun*
Remember that the ending of **conductor** is **-or**.
TIP: a conductor directs an orchestra.

confectionery *noun*
The ending of **confectionery** is spelled **-ery**.

confer *verb*
RULE: If a verb ends with a single vowel plus a consonant, and the stress is at the end of the word (as in *refer*), double the last letter when adding **-ing** or **-ed**: confers, conferring, conferred.

RELATED WORD: conference *noun*

confetti *noun*
Spell **confetti** with one **f** and a double **t**: it is an Italian word.

confident *adjective*
❗ Do not confuse **confident** with **confidant**. **Confident** means 'believing that you can do things well' (*a confident, outgoing girl*), whereas **confidant** means 'a person that you tell private and secret things to' (*she was a close confidant of the princess*).

conjuror *noun*
Conjuror can also be spelled **conjurer**; both are correct.

connection *noun*
Connection can also be spelled **connexion**: both are correct.

connoisseur *noun*
Remember that **connoisseur** has a double **n** and a double **s**, with **-oi-** between them: it is a French word.

conscience *noun*
Remember that **conscience** has **-sci-** in the middle.

conscious *adjective*
Spell **conscious** with **-sci-** in the middle.

consensus *noun*
Remember that **consensus** and the related word **consensual** are spelled with **-sen-** in the middle.

consequence *noun*
Remember that **consequence** ends with **-ence**.
RELATED WORD: consequent *adjective*

conservatory *noun* (plural **conservatories**)
The ending of **conservatory** is spelled **-ory**.

consistent *adjective*
The ending of **consistent** is spelled **-ent**.
RELATED WORD: consistency *noun*

consonant *noun and adjective*
The ending of **consonant** is spelled **-ant**.

consortium *noun*
The plural of **consortium** can be spelled either **consortia** (as in the original Latin) or **consortiums**.

conspicuous *adjective*
Remember that the ending of **conspicuous** is spelled **-uous**.

consultant *noun*
The ending of **consultant** is **-ant**.

consummate *verb and adjective*
Spell **consummate** with a double **m**.

contemporary *adjective and noun* (plural **contemporaries**)
The ending of **contemporary** is spelled **-porary**.

contemptible *adjective*
Remember that **contemptible** ends with **-ible**.

continent *noun*
Remember that **continent** ends with **-ent**. It is often spelled with a capital **C** when referring to Europe (*clubs sprang up in Britain and on the Continent*).

continuous *adjective*
Remember that **continuous** is spelled with a **u** before the **-ous** ending.

contractor *noun*
The ending of **contractor** is spelled **-or**.

control *noun and verb*

> **RULE:** Double the **l** when adding endings which begin with a vowel to words which end in a vowel plus **l** (as in *travel*): **controls, controlling, controlled**.

controversy *noun* (plural **controversies**)
Remember that **controversy** is spelled with **-ro-** in the middle.
TIP: cont**ro**versy arouses **r**eally **o**pposing views.
RELATED WORD: controversial *adjective*

convalesce *verb*
Remember that **convalesce** and the related word **convalescent** are spelled with **-esc-** after the **l**.

convenience *noun*
Spell **convenience** with **-ven-** in the middle; the ending is **-ience**.
RELATED WORD: convenient *adjective*

convertible *adjective and noun*
Spell **convertible** with **-ible** at the end.

cooperate *verb*
Cooperate and its related words (such as **cooperative**) may also be spelled with a hyphen: **co-operate, co-operative**.

coordinate *verb and noun*
Remember that **coordinate** and its related words (such as **coordination**) may also be spelled with a hyphen: **co-ordinate, co-ordination**.

cord *noun*
! Do not confuse **cord** with **chord**. See **CHORD**.

corduroy *noun*
Spell **corduroy** with **-dur-** in the middle.

coronary *adjective and noun*
Remember that **coronary** ends with **-ary**.

correspondence *noun*
Spell **correspondence** with a double **r** and **-ence** at the end.
RELATED WORD: correspondent *noun*

corridor *noun*
Remember that **corridor** ends with **-dor**.
TIP: the corri**dor** led to a **dor**mitory.

corroborate *verb*
Spell **corroborate** with a double **r** and then **-obor-**.

cosmopolitan *adjective and noun*
Spell **cosmopolitan** with **cosmo-** at the beginning and **-an** at the end.

council *noun*
! Do not confuse **council** with **counsel**. **Council** means 'a group of people who manage an area or advise on something' (*the city council*), whereas **counsel** means 'advice' or 'advise' (*we counselled him on estate planning*).

councillor *noun*
Remember that **councillor** has a double **l** (the spelling **councilor** is American).

counsel *verb*
RULE: Double the **l** when adding endings which begin with a vowel to words which end in a vowel plus **l** (as in *travel*): counsels, counselling, counselled.

! Do not confuse **counsel** with **council**. See **COUNCIL**.

counsellor *noun*
Remember that **counsellor** has a double **l** (the spelling **counselor** is American).

counterfeit *adjective and verb*
Spell **counterfeit** with **-eit** at the end.

coupé *noun*
Coupé is usually written with an accent on the **e**, as in the original French.

courageous *adjective*
RULE: Keep the final **-e** when adding **-ous** to *courage* to make sure that **courageous** is pronounced with a soft *-ge-* sound: courageous.

courgette *noun*
Remember that **courgette** begins with **cou-** and that the ending is **-gette**.

course *noun and verb*
! Do not confuse **course** with **coarse**. See **COARSE**.

courteous *adjective*
Remember that **courteous** and the related word **courtesy** begin with **cou-**.

couscous *noun*
Couscous should be spelled with **cous-** at the beginning and **-cous** at the end (it is an Arabic word).

covet *verb*

> **RULE:** Do not double the final consonant when adding endings which begin with a vowel to a word which ends in a vowel plus a consonant, if the stress is not at the end of the word (as in *target*): covets, coveting, coveted.

creator *noun*
The ending of **creator** is spelled **-or**.

crèche *noun*
Crèche is a French word; it can also be spelled **creche**, without the accent on the first **e**.

credence *noun*
Spell **credence** with three single **e**'s.

credible *adjective*
Remember that the ending of **credible** is **-ible**.

crematorium *noun*
The plural of **crematorium** can be spelled either **crematoria** (like the original Latin) or **crematoriums**.

crêpe *noun*
Crêpe is a French word, and is usually spelled with an accent (called a circumflex) on the first **e**, although **crepe** is also correct.

crescendo *noun* (plural **crescendos**)
Spell **crescendo** with **-sc-** in the middle.

crescent *noun*
Remember that **crescent** has **-sc-** in the middle.
TIP: the **s**ilver **c**urve of the cre**sc**ent moon.

crisis *noun*

> **RULE:** Make the plural by changing the **-is** ending to **-es**: crises.

criterion *noun*
To make the plural of **criterion**, change the **-on** ending to **-a** (as in the original Greek): criteria.

criticize, criticise *verb*
Remember that **criticize** and the related word **criticism** have a **c** before the final **i** as well as one at the beginning.

crocodile *noun*
Spell **crocodile** with **-co-** in the middle.

croissant *noun*
Remember that **croissant** begins with **croi-**, followed by a double **s**; it is a French word.

crudités *plural noun*
Crudités is a French word and is usually spelled with an accent on the **e**.

cruel *adjective*

> **RULE:** Double the **l** when adding endings which begin with a vowel to words which end in a vowel plus **l**: crueller, cruellest.

RELATED WORD: cruelty *noun*

cubicle *noun*
Remember that the ending of **cubicle** is spelled **-cle**.

cue *noun and verb* (**cues, cueing or cuing, cued**)
Cueing is usually spelled with an **e**, although **cuing** is also correct.
‼ Do not confuse **cue** with **queue**. **Cue** means 'a signal for action' (*the announcement was a cue for the crowd to gather*) or 'a long wooden rod', whereas **queue** means 'a line of people or vehicles' (*I joined the end of the queue*).

culinary *adjective*
Remember that the ending of **culinary** is spelled **-ary**.

culottes *plural noun*
Spell **culottes** with one **l** and a double **t**.

cumin *noun*
Cumin can also be spelled **cummin**, with a double **m**: both are correct.

curator *noun*
The ending of **curator** is spelled **-or**.

curb *verb and noun*
❗ Do not confuse **curb** with **kerb**. **Curb** means 'control or limit something' (*she promised to curb her temper*) or 'a thing that controls or limits', whereas **kerb** means 'the stone edging of a pavement' (the spelling **curb** in this sense is American).

curiosity *noun* (plural curiosities)
Spell **curiosity** with **-os-** in the middle.

current *adjective and noun*
❗ Do not confuse **current** with **currant**. **Current** means 'happening now' (*current events*) or 'a flow of water, air, or electricity' (*strong ocean currents*), whereas

currant means 'a dried grape' (*currant cake*).
RELATED WORD: currency *noun*

curriculum *noun*
The plural of **curriculum** can be spelled either **curricula** (as in the original Latin) or **curriculums**.

curriculum vitae *noun*
Curriculum vitae is a Latin phrase meaning 'course of life'. The plural is made by changing the ending of **curriculum** from **-um** to **-a**: curricula vitae.

cursor *noun*
Remember that **cursor** ends with **-or**.

curvaceous *adjective*
The ending of **curvaceous** is spelled **-ceous**.

cygnet *noun*
❗ Do not confuse **cygnet** with **signet**. A **cygnet** is a young swan, whereas **signet** is usually found in the phrase **signet ring**, which is a ring with letters or a design on it.

cylinder *noun*
Spell **cylinder** with **cyl-** at the beginning and **-er** at the end.

c

Dd

dachshund *noun*
Remember that **dachshund** begins with **dachs-**; it is a German word.

daffodil *noun*
Spell **daffodil** with a double **f** and a single **l**.

daiquiri *noun* (plural **daiquiris**)
Spell **daiquiri** with **daiq-** at the beginning.

dairy *noun* (plural **dairies**)
! Do not confuse **dairy** with **diary**. **Dairy** means 'a place for storing milk', whereas **diary** means 'a book for keeping a daily record'.

Dalmatian *noun*
Remember that the ending of **Dalmatian** is spelled **-tian**; the dog is named after *Dalmatia* (a region of Croatia).

debatable *adjective*
Remember that **debatable** ends with **-able**.

debit *noun and verb*

> **RULE:** Do not double the final consonant when adding endings which begin with a vowel to a word which ends in a vowel plus a consonant, if the stress is not at the end of the word (as in *target*): debits, debiting, debited.

debut *noun and verb*
Debut can also be spelled **début**, with an accent on the **e** (as in the original French).

decaffeinated *adjective*
Spell **decaffeinated** with a double **f**, then **-ei-**; it does not follow the rule **i** before **e** except after **c**.

deceive *verb*

> **RULE: i** before **e** except after **c** (as in *receive*).

> **RELATED WORD: deceit** *noun*

decennial *adjective*
Spell **decennial** with a double **n**.

decor *noun*
Decor is a French word and can also be spelled **décor**, with an accent on the **e**.

decorator *noun*
Remember that **decorator** ends with **-or**.

deductible *adjective*
The ending of **deductible** is spelled **-ible**.

defence *noun*
The ending of **defence** is spelled **-ence** (the spelling **defense** is American).

defendant *noun*
Remember that **defendant** ends in **-ant**.

defensible *adjective*
Spell **defensible** with **-ible** at the end.

defer *verb*

> **RULE:** If a verb ends with a single vowel plus a consonant, and the

stress is at the end of the word (as in *refer*), double the last letter when adding **-ing** or **-ed**: defers, deferring, deferred.

! Do not confuse **defer** with **differ**. *See* **DIFFER**.

definite *adjective*
Remember that **definite** ends with **-Ite**.
RELATED WORD: definitely *adverb*

defuse *verb*
! Do not confuse **defuse** with **diffuse**. **Defuse** means 'make a situation less tense or dangerous' (*talks were held to defuse the crisis*), while **diffuse** means 'spread over a wide area' (*this early language probably diffused across the world*).

defy *verb*

> **RULE:** If a word ends in a consonant plus **-y**, change the **-y** to an **-i** before adding any ending (unless the ending already begins with an **-i**): defies, defying, defied.

RELATED WORD: defiance *noun*

deign *verb*
Remember that the ending of **deign** is spelled **-ign**.

delicatessen *noun*
Spell **delicatessen** with a double **s**.
TIP: spicy **s**alami from the delicate**ss**en.

demeanour *noun*
Remember that **demeanour** ends with **-our** (the spelling **demeanor** is American).

denigrate *verb*
Spell **denigrate** with an **i** after the **n**.

denominator *noun*
Spell **denominator** with **-or** at the end.

denouement *noun*
Denouement can also be spelled **dénouement**, with an accent on the first **e** (as in the original French).

deodorant *noun*
Remember that **deodorant** is spelled with **-odor-** in the middle; the ending is **-ant**.

deodorize, deodorise *verb*
Spell **deodorize** with **-odor-** in the middle.

dependant *noun*
The noun **dependant** can also be spelled **dependent**: both spellings are correct, although **dependent** is more common in American English.

dependent *adjective*
Remember that the ending of the adjective **dependent** is always spelled **-ent**.

deposit *verb*

> **RULE:** Do not double the final consonant when adding endings which begin with a vowel to a word which ends in a vowel plus a consonant, if the stress is not at the end of the word (as in *target*): deposits, depositing, deposited.

RELATED WORD: depositor *noun*

descend *verb*
Remember that **descend** and the related word **descent** are spelled with **-sc-** in the middle.
RELATED WORD: descendant *noun*

desert *noun and verb*
! Do not confuse **desert** with **dessert**. **Desert** means 'a waterless, empty area' (*the Sahara Desert*) or 'leave someone or something' (*he deserted her for another woman*), whereas **dessert** means 'the sweet course of a meal' (*an ice cream dessert*).

desiccated *adjective*
Remember that **desiccated** is spelled with a single **s** and a double **c**.

desirable *adjective*
The ending of **desirable** is spelled **-able**.

despair *verb*
Remember that the beginning of **despair** is spelled **des-**.

desperate *adjective*
Spell **desperate** with **-per-** in the middle.
TIP: **per**haps he was des**per**ate to escape.

despise *verb*
Unlike most verbs ending in **-ise**, **despise** cannot be spelled with an **-ize** ending. *See centre pages for other verbs that always end in* **-ise**.

despondent *adjective*
Remember that the ending of **despondent** is spelled **-ent**.

dessert *noun*
! Do not confuse **dessert** with **desert**. *See* **DESERT**.

destructible *adjective*
The ending of **destructible** is spelled **-ible**.

detach *verb*
The ending of **detach** should be spelled **-ach**. *See centre pages for advice on words ending in* **-ach** *or* **-atch**.

detector *noun*
Remember that **detector** ends with **-or**.

deter *verb*

> **RULE:** If a verb ends with a single vowel plus a consonant, and the stress is at the end of the word (as in *refer*), double the last letter when adding endings which begin with a vowel: deters, deterring, deterred.

RELATED WORD: deterrent *noun*

develop *verb* (develops, developing, developed)
Remember that the ending of **develop** is just **-op**.
RELATED WORD: development *noun*

devise *verb*
Unlike most verbs ending in **-ise**, **devise** cannot be spelled with an **-ize** ending. *See centre pages for other verbs that always end in* **-ise**.

dexterous *adjective*
Dexterous can also be spelled **dextrous**, without the second **e**; both are correct.

diagnosis *noun*

> **RULE:** Make the plural of **diagnosis** by changing the **-is** ending to **-es**: diagnoses.

dial *verb and noun*

> **RULE:** Double the **l** when adding endings which begin with a vowel to words which end in a vowel plus **l** (as in *travel*): dials, dialling, dialled.

dialogue *noun*
The ending of **dialogue** is spelled **-gue** (the spelling **dialog** is American).

diameter *noun*
Remember that **diameter** ends in **-meter**.

diaphragm *noun*
Remember that **diaphragm** has a **g** before the **m**, although it is not heard when you say the word.

diarrhoea *noun*
Spell **diarrhoea** with a double **r**; the ending is **-hoea** (the spelling **diarrhea** is American).

diary *noun* (plural **diaries**)
! Do not confuse **diary** with **dairy**. See **DAIRY**.

dictionary *noun* (plural **dictionaries**)
Remember that **dictionary** is spelled with **-ar-** after the **n**.
TIP: a dictionary is an **a**lphabetical **r**eference book.

die *verb*

> **RULE:** When a verb ends with **-ie**, change the **-ie** ending to **-y** when adding **-ing**: **dies**, **dying**, **died**.

diesel *noun*

> **RULE:** **i** before **e** except after **c** (as in *thief*).

dietitian *noun*
Dietitian can also be spelled **dietician**: both are correct.

differ *verb*
! Do not confuse **differ** with **defer**. **Differ** means 'be different' (*our tastes differ, especially in cars*), whereas **defer** means 'put something off until later' (*I deferred the decision until May*).
RELATED WORDS: **difference** *noun*, **different** *adjective*

diffuse *verb and adjective*
! Do not confuse **diffuse** with **defuse**. See **DEFUSE**.

digit *noun*
Spell **digit** with **-git** at the end.

digress *verb*
Spell **digress** with one **g** and a double **s**.

dilemma *noun*
Remember that **dilemma** is spelled with a single **l** and a double **m**.

dimension *noun*
Spell **dimension** with **-sion** at the end.

dinghy *noun* (plural **dinghies**)
Remember that **dinghy** is spelled with **gh** after the **n**.

dinosaur *noun*
Spell **dinosaur** with an **o** after the **n**; the ending is **-saur**.

diphtheria *noun*
Remember that **diphtheria** is spelled with **ph** then **th** in the middle.

director *noun*
The ending of **director** is spelled **-or**.

disappear *verb*
Spell **disappear** and the related word **disappearance** with one **s** and a double **p**.

disappoint *verb*
Remember that **disappoint** and the related word **disappointment** are spelled with one **s** and a double **p**.

disapprove *verb*
Spell **disapprove** and the related word **disapproval** with one **s** and a double **p**.

disastrous *adjective*
Remember that **disastrous**, although it is related to *disaster*, is spelled **-str-** in the middle.

disc *noun*
Generally speaking, **disc** is spelled with a **c** at the end (the spelling **disk** is American). However, the spelling for computer-related senses is usually **disk**: *floppy disk*, *disk drive*, etc.

d

discern *verb*
Remember that **discern** is spelled with **-sc-** in the middle.
TIP: I di**sc**erned **s**ix **c**ats in the garden.

disciple *noun*
Spell **disciple** with **-sc-** in the middle and **-iple** at the end.

discipline *noun and verb*
Remember that **discipline** is spelled with **-sc-** in the middle.

discreet *adjective*
❗ Do not confuse **discreet** with **discrete**. **Discreet** means 'careful not to attract attention' (*we made some discreet inquiries*), whereas **discrete** means 'separate and distinct' (*a series of discrete tasks*).

discuss *verb*
Spell **discuss** and the related word **discussion** with **dis-** at the beginning, followed by a double **s**.

disease *noun*
The ending of **disease** is spelled **-ease**.

disfavour *noun*
Remember that **disfavour** ends with **-our** (the spelling **disfavor** is American).

dishonour *noun and verb*
Remember that **dishonour** ends with **-our** (the spelling **dishonor** is American).

disinfectant *noun*
Spell **disinfectant** with **-ant** at the end.

disinterested *adjective*
❗ Do not confuse **disinterested** with **uninterested**. **Disinterested** means 'treating everyone equally; impartial' (*a banker should give disinterested advice*), while **uninterested** means 'not interested' (*a man uninterested in money*).

dispatch *verb and noun*
Dispatch can also be spelled **despatch**, with an **e**; both are correct. The ending is spelled **-atch**. *See centre pages for advice on words ending in* **-atch** *or* **-ach**.

dispel *verb*

> **RULE:** Double the **l** when adding endings which begin with a vowel to words which end in a vowel plus **l** (as in *travel*): **dispels**, **dispelling**, **dispelled**.

dissatisfied *adjective*
Spell **dissatisfied** and the related word **dissatisfaction** with a double **s**.

dissect *verb*
Remember that **dissect** and the related word **dissection** have a double **s**.
TIP: she di**ss**ected **s**everal **s**pecimens.

distil *verb*

> **RULE:** Double the **l** when adding endings which begin with a vowel to words which end in a vowel plus **l** (as in *travel*): **distils**, **distilling**, **distilled**.

RELATED WORD: distillation *noun*

distraught *adjective*
Remember that the ending of **distraught** is spelled **-aught**.

distributor *noun*
The ending of **distributor** is spelled **-or**.

divisible *adjective*
Remember that the ending of **divisible** is spelled **-ible**.

domino *noun*
The plural of **domino** is made by adding **-es**: **dominoes**.

doughnut *noun*
The beginning of **doughnut** is spelled **dough-** (the spelling **donut** is American).

draft *noun and verb*
❗ Do not confuse **draft** with **draught**. **Draft** means 'a first version of a piece of writing' or 'make a first version of a piece of writing' (*I drafted a letter of complaint*), whereas **draught** chiefly means 'a current of air' (*heavy curtains cut out draughts*). **Draft** is the American spelling for both senses.

draw *verb and noun*
❗ Do not confuse **draw** with **drawer**. As a noun, **draw** chiefly means 'an even score at the end of a game' (*the match ended in a goalless draw*), whereas **drawer** means 'a sliding storage compartment' (*a cutlery drawer*).

drily *adverb*
Drily can also be spelled **dryly**, with a **y**; both are correct.

drunkenness *noun*
Remember that **drunkenness** is spelled with a double **n** (it is made up of the word **drunken** plus the ending **-ness**).

dry *adjective and verb* (**dries, drying, dried**)

> **RULE:** If a word ends in a consonant plus **-y**, change the **-y** to an **-i** before adding any ending (unless the ending already begins with an **-i**): **drier, driest**.

RELATED WORD: **dryness** *noun*

dryer *noun*
The noun **dryer** can also be spelled **drier**; both are correct.

dual *adjective*
❗ Do not confuse **dual** with **duel**. **Dual** means 'having two parts or aspects' (*the dual role of proprietor/manager*), whereas **duel** means 'a fight or contest between two people' (*he challenged me to a duel*).

duel *noun and verb* (**duels, duelling, duelled**)
❗ Do not confuse **duel** with **dual**. See **DUAL**.

duffel *adjective*
Duffel (as in *duffel bag* and *duffel coat*) can also be spelled **duffle**; both are correct.

duress *noun*
Spell **duress** with one **r** and a double **s**.

dwarf *noun and verb*
The plural of **dwarf** can be spelled either **dwarfs** or **dwarves**.

dye *noun and verb*

> **RULE:** Verbs ending in **-oe**, **-ee**, and **-ye** keep the final **-e** when adding **-ing**: **dyes, dyeing, dyed**.

dyke *noun*
Dyke can also be spelled **dike**; both are correct.

dysfunctional *adjective*
Remember that **dysfunctional** begins with **dys-**. It belongs to a group of words based on the Greek word *dus-* meaning 'bad' or 'difficult'. Other words that begin with **dys-** include *dysentery* and *dyslexia*.

Ee

early *adjective*

> **RULE:** If an adjective ends in a consonant plus **y**, change the **y** to **i** when adding **-er** or **-est**: earlier, earliest.

earnest *adjective*
Remember that **earnest** begins with **ea-**.
TIP: make **ea**rnest **e**fforts to be active.

earring *noun*
Spell **earring** with a double **r**.

easy *adjective*

> **RULE:** If a word ends in a consonant plus **-y**, change the **-y** to an **-i** before adding any ending (unless the ending already begins with an **-i**): easier, easiest.

RELATED WORDS: easily *adverb*, easiness *noun*

eccentric *adjective*
Spell **eccentric** and the related word **eccentricity** with a double **c**.

echo *noun and verb* (echoes, echoing, echoed)
The plural of **echo** is made by adding **-es**: echoes.

eclair *noun*
Eclair can also be spelled **éclair**, with an accent on the **e** (as in the original French).

ecstasy *noun*
Remember that the ending of **ecstasy** is **-asy**.

eczema *noun*
Spell **eczema** with an **e** after the **z**.

edible *adjective*
Spell **edible** with **-ible** at the end.

effect *noun and verb*
❗ Do not confuse **effect** with **affect**. *See* **AFFECT**.

effervesce *verb*
Remember that **effervesce** has a double **f**; the ending is **-sce**.
RELATED WORD: effervescent *adjective*

-efy
*See centre pages for words ending with **-efy** and **-ify**.*

eighth *adjective*
Remember that **eighth** is spelled with **-hth** at the end.
TIP: Sam **h**oped **t**hat **h**e wouldn't finish eig**hth**.

elaborate *adjective and verb*
Spell **elaborate** with **-bor-** in the middle.

electable *adjective*
The ending of **electable** is spelled **-able**.

elicit *verb*
❗ Do not confuse **elicit** with **illicit**. *See* **ILLICIT**.

eligible *adjective*
Remember that the ending of **eligible** is spelled **-ible**.

elite *noun*
> **Elite** can also be spelled **élite**, with an accent on the **e** (as in the original French).

elusive *adjective*
> ! Do not confuse **elusive** with **illusive**. **Elusive** means 'hard to find, catch, or achieve' (*what I was looking for proved elusive*), whereas **illusive** means 'not real, although seeming to be' (*the illusive nature of the material world*).

email *noun and verb*
> **Email** can also be spelled **e-mail**, with a hyphen; the spelling with the hyphen is now less common.

embargo *noun and verb*
(**embargoes**, **embargoing**, **embargoed**)
> The plural of **embargo** is made by adding **-es**: embargoes.

embarrass *verb*
> Remember that **embarrass** and the related word **embarrassment** have a double **r** and a double **s**.

emit *verb*

> **RULE:** If a verb ends with a single vowel plus a consonant, and the stress is at the end of the word (as in *refer*), double the last letter when adding **-ing** or **-ed**: emits, emitting, emitted.

emphasize, emphasise *verb*
> Remember that **emphasize** is spelled with **-phas-** in the middle.
> **RELATED WORD:** emphasis *noun*

enamelled *adjective*
> Spell **enamelled** with two **l**'s (the spelling **enameled** is American).

enamoured *adjective*
> Spell **enamoured** with **-our-** in the middle (the spelling **enamored** is American).

-ence
> *See centre pages for words ending in -ence, -ency, and -ent.*

encumbrance *noun*
> Remember that **encumbrance** ends with **-brance**.

encyclopedia *noun*
> **Encyclopedia** can also be spelled **encyclopaedia**, with **-ae-** after the **p**, but this is less common.

endeavour *verb and noun*
> Remember that **endeavour** ends with **-our** (the spelling **endeavor** is American).

enfranchise *verb*
> Unlike most verbs ending in **-ise**, **enfranchise** cannot be spelled with an **-ize** ending. *See centre pages for other verbs that always end in -ise.*

enmity *noun*
> Remember that **enmity** is spelled with the **n** before the **m**.
> **TIP:** their e**n**mity drove them to **n**asty **m**easures.

enquire *verb*
> **Enquire** and the related word **enquiry** can also be spelled **inquire** and **inquiry**; there is no real difference between them in meaning, but the spellings **inquire** and **inquiry** are more common in American English.

enrol *verb*

> **RULE:** Double the **l** when adding endings which begin with a vowel to words which end in a vowel plus **l** (as in *travel*): enrols, enrolling, enrolled.

> **RELATED WORD:** enrolment *noun*

ensure *verb*
> ! In more general senses, **ensure** and **insure** mean the same thing, 'make certain that something will happen': *ensure that accurate*

records are kept or insure that *accurate records are kept.* However, only **insure** means 'provide compensation for damage to property or if a person dies': *the table should be insured for £2,500.*

enterprise *noun*
Remember that **enterprise** ends with **-ise**.

enthral *verb*

> **RULE:** Double the **l** when adding endings which begin with a vowel to words which end in a vowel plus **l** (as in *travel*): enthrals, enthralling, enthralled.

entrepreneur *noun*
Spell **entrepreneur** (a French word) with **-eur** at the end.

envelop *verb* (envelops, enveloping, enveloped)
! Do not confuse **envelop** with **envelope**. **Envelop** means 'cover or surround something completely' (*the mist seemed to envelop the boat*), whereas **envelope** means 'a paper container for a letter' (*a stamped addressed envelope*).

environment *noun*
Remember that **environment** has an **n** before the **m**.
TIP: protect the **n**atural **m**agnificence of the enviro**nm**ent.

enzyme *noun*
The ending of **enzyme** is spelled **-zyme**.

epitome *noun*
Remember that **epitome** ends **-tome**.

equal *verb* and *adjective*

> **RULE:** Double the **l** when adding endings which begin with a vowel to words which end in a vowel plus

l (as in *travel*): equals, equalling, equalled.

equip *verb*

> **RULE:** If a verb ends with a single vowel plus a consonant, and the stress is at the end of the word (as in *refer*), double the last letter when adding **-ing** or **-ed**: equips, equipping, equipped.

RELATED WORD: equipment *noun*

-er
See centre pages for words ending in **-er**, **-ar**, *and* **-or**.

erroneous *adjective*
Spell **erroneous** with a double **r**; the ending is **-eous**.

-ery
See centre pages for words ending with **-ery**, **-ary**, *and* **-ory**.

escalator *noun*
The ending of **escalator** is spelled **-or**.

especially *adverb*
Remember that **especially** is spelled with a double **l** at the end.

espresso *noun* (plural espressos)
Remember that **espresso** begins with **es-**. The spelling **expresso** is not found in the original Italian and is incorrect.

estuary *noun*
Remember that **estuary** has **-tua-** in the middle.

> **RULE:** Make the plural of words that end in a consonant plus **-y** by changing the **-y** to **-ies**: estuaries.

euro *noun*

> **RULE:** The plural of **euro** is made in the usual way, by adding **-s**: euros.

euthanasia *noun*
Spell **euthanasia** with **-than-** in the middle.

evaporate *verb*
Remember that **evaporate** and the related word **evaporation** are spelled with **-por-** in the middle.

evidence *noun and verb*
Spell **evidence** with **evi-** at the beginning.
RELATED WORD: evident *adjective*

exaggerate *verb*
Spell **exaggerate** and the related word **exaggeration** with a double **g** and a single **r**.
TIP: a bra**gg**er always exa**gg**erates.

exceed *verb*
Remember that **exceed** ends with **-eed**. *See centre pages for other verbs that end in* **-cede** *or* **-ceed**.

excel *verb*

> **RULE:** Double the **l** when adding endings which begin with a vowel to words which end in a vowel plus **l** (as in *travel*): ex**cels**, ex**celling**, ex**celled**.

RELATED WORD: excellent *adjective*

except *verb and preposition*
❗ Do not confuse **accept** with **except**. *See* **ACCEPT**.

excerpt *noun and verb*
Remember that **excerpt** has a **p** before the **t**, although it is not heard when you say the word.

excess *noun*
Spell **excess** with **exc-** at the beginning; the ending is **-ess**.

excise *verb*
Unlike most verbs ending in **-ise**, **excise** cannot be spelled with an **-ize** ending. *See centre pages for other verbs that always end in* **-ise**.

excite *verb* (excites, exciting, excited)
Remember that **excite** begins with **exc-**.
RELATED WORDS: excitable *adjective*, excitement *noun*

exercise *noun and verb*
Unlike most verbs ending in **-ise**, **exercise** cannot be spelled with an **-ize** ending. *See centre pages for other verbs that always end in* **-ise**.
❗ Do not confuse **exercise** with **exorcize**. *See* **EXORCIZE**.

exhaust *verb and noun*
Remember that **exhaust** is spelled with an **h** after the **x**.

exhibit *noun and verb*
Spell **exhibit** with an **h** after the **x**.
RELATED WORDS: exhibition *noun*, exhibitor *noun*

exhilarate *verb*
Remember that **exhilarate** and the related word **exhilaration** have an **h** after the **x**.

existence *noun*
The ending of **existence** is spelled **-ence**.
RELATED WORD: existent *adjective*

exorcize, exorcise *verb*
❗ Do not confuse **exorcize** with **exercise**. **Exorcize** means 'drive out an evil spirit' (*a magic formula used to exorcise evil spirits*), whereas **exercise** means 'carry out physical activity to get fitter' (*she exercised every day*) or 'use a right or power' (*control is exercised by the Council*).

expedient *adjective and noun*
Spell **expedient** with **-ent** at the end.

expel *verb*

> **RULE:** Double the **l** when adding endings which begin with a vowel

to words which end in a vowel plus **l** (as in *travel*): expels, expelling, expelled.

expense *noun*
Remember that **expense** ends with **-ense**.

explanation *noun*
Remember that **explanation** is spelled with **-lan-** in the middle.

extraneous *adjective*
Remember that **extraneous** begins with **extra-** and that it ends with **-eous**.

extraordinary *adjective*
Spell **extraordinary** with **extra-** at the beginning (it is made up of the words **extra** and **ordinary**).

extreme *adjective and noun*
Remember that the ending of **extreme** is spelled **-eme**.

extrovert *noun and adjective*
Spell **extrovert** with an **o** in the middle.
TIP: an extrovert is outgoing.

eye *noun and verb* (eyes, eyeing or eying, eyed)
Eyeing is usually spelled with an **e**, although **eying** is also correct.

f-
The sound *f-* is sometimes spelled *ph-* (as in *phenomenon*). *If you cannot find the word you are looking for here, check words that begin with* **ph-**.

facetious *adjective*
Remember that **facetious** ends with **-tious**.

facility *noun* (plural **facilities**)
Spell **facility** and the related word **facilitate** with one **c** and one **l**.

Fahrenheit *noun*
Fahrenheit should be spelled with a capital **F**, then **-ahr-**; the ending is **-heit**. It is named after the German physicist Gabriel Daniel *Fahrenheit*.

faint *adjective, noun, and verb*
! Do not confuse **faint** with **feint**. **Faint** means 'only just able to be seen, heard, or smelled' (*the faint murmur of voices*) or 'lose consciousness', while **feint** means 'a mock attack' or 'make a deceptive movement' (*I feinted to the right, then moved to the left*).

fair *adjective*
! Do not confuse **fair** with **fare**. *See* **FARE**.

fajitas *plural noun*
Remember that **fajitas** is spelled with a **j** in the middle; it is spoken like an *h* because it is a Spanish word.

falafel *noun*
Falafel (a word of Arabic origin) can also be spelled **felafel**; both are correct.

fallible *adjective*
Remember that **fallible** has a double **l** and ends with **-ible**.

familiar *adjective*
Remember that **familiar** is spelled with a single **l**.

fare *noun and verb*
! Do not confuse **fare** with **fair**. **Fare** means 'money paid by passengers' (*a bus fare*) or 'progress in a particular way' (*the party fared badly in the election*), whereas **fair** mainly means 'treating people equally; just' (*a fair deal*) or is used to describe hair as being light-coloured.

fascinate *verb*
Remember that **fascinate** and the related word **fascination** are spelled with a **c** after the **s**.

fascism *noun*
Spell **fascism** and the related word **fascist** with a **c** after the **s**.

fatigue *noun and verb*

> **RULE:** Drop the final silent **-e** when adding **-ing** or **-ed**: fatigues, fatiguing, fatigued.

faun *noun*
! Do not confuse **faun** and **fawn**. *See* **FAWN**.

favour *verb and noun*

Remember that **favour** ends with
-our (the spelling **favor** is
American).
RELATED WORD: favourite *adjective*

fawn *noun and verb*

! Do not confuse **fawn** with **faun**.
Fawn means 'a young deer', 'a light
brown colour', or 'try to gain
someone's approval by flattering
them' (*people fawn over you when
you're famous*); **faun** means 'a
Roman god that is part man, part
goat'.

feasible *adjective*

The ending of **feasible** is spelled
-ible.

February *noun*

Remember that **February** has two
r's; one after the **b** and one near
the end.
TIP: February was really rainy.

feign *verb*

Spell **feign** with **fei-** at the
beginning; the ending is **-gn**.

feint *noun and verb*

! Do not confuse **feint** with **faint**. *See*
FAINT.

fervent *adjective*

The ending of **fervent** is spelled
-ent.

fervour *noun*

Remember that **fervour** ends with
-our (the spelling **fervor** is
American).

fête *noun and verb*

Fête (a French word) is usually
spelled with an accent (called a
circumflex) on the first **e**, although
fete is also correct.

fetid *adjective*

Fetid can also be spelled **foetid**,
with an **o** before the **e**: both are

correct, although **fetid** is more
common.

fettuccine *plural noun*

Spell **fettuccine** with a double
t and a double **c**; it is an Italian
word.

fetus *noun* (plural **fetuses**)

Fetus can also be spelled **foetus**,
with an **o** before the **e**; **fetus** is the
spelling used by scientists.

fiancé *noun*

Fiancé (a French word) can also be
spelled **fiance**, without an accent
on the **e**. Similarly, the feminine
form can be spelled **fiancée** or
fiancee.

fiasco *noun* (plural **fiascos**)

Spell **fiasco** (an Italian word) with
fia- at the beginning.

fibre *noun*

Remember that **fibre** ends with **-re**
(the spelling **fiber** is American).

fictitious *adjective*

Spell **fictitious** with **-tious** at the
end.

fidget *verb and noun*

> **RULE:** Do not double the final
> consonant when adding endings
> which begin with a vowel to a
> word which ends in a vowel plus a
> consonant, if the stress is not at
> the end of the word (as in *target*):
> fidgets, fidgeting, fidgeted.

field *noun and verb*

> **RULE:** i before e except after c (as
> in *thief*).

fiend *noun*

> **RULE:** i before e except after c (as
> in *thief*).

fierce *adjective*

> **RULE: i** before **e** except after **c** (as in *thief*).

fillet *noun and verb*

> **RULE:** Do not double the final consonant when adding endings which begin with a vowel to a word which ends in a vowel plus a consonant, if the stress is not at the end of the word (as in *target*): **fillets, filleting, filleted.**

filo *noun*
> **Filo** can also be spelled **phyllo** (it comes from Greek *phullo* 'leaf').

final *adjective and noun*
> ! Do not confuse **final** with **finale. Final** means 'coming at the end; last' or 'the last game in a series, to decide the overall winner' (*the World Cup final*), whereas **finale** means 'the last part of a piece of music, an entertainment, or a public event' (*the festival ended with a grand finale*).

finesse *noun*
> Spell **finesse** with one **n** and a double **s**.
> **TIP:** fi**n**esse **n**eeds **s**ubtle **s**kill.

fish *noun and verb*
> The normal plural of **fish** is **fish** (*I caught two fish*). When you want to talk about different kinds of fish, however, you should use **fishes**: *freshwater fishes of the British Isles*.

fjord *noun*
> **Fjord** (a Norwegian word) can also be spelled **fiord**: both are correct.

flaccid *adjective*
> Spell **flaccid** with a double **c**.

flair *noun*
> ! Do not confuse **flair** with **flare. Flair** means 'a natural ability or talent' (*she had a flair for*

languages*), whereas **flare** means 'burn suddenly' or 'become wider' (*a flared skirt*).

flambé *adjective and verb* (**flambés, flambéed, flambéing**)
> **Flambé** is a French word and is usually spelled with an accent on the **e**.

flamingo *noun*
> The plural of **flamingo** can be spelled **flamingos** or **flamingoes**.

flare *verb and noun*
> ! Do not confuse **flare** with **flair** See **FLAIR**.

flavour *noun and verb*
> Remember that **flavour** ends with **-our** (the spelling **flavor** is American).

fledgling *noun*
> **Fledgling** can also be spelled **fledgeling**: both are correct.

flexible *adjective*
> The ending of **flexible** is spelled **-ible**.

flippant *adjective*
> Remember that the ending of **flippant** is **-ant**.

flotation *noun*
> Remember that **flotation** begins with **flot-**.

flotilla *noun*
> Spell **flotilla** with one **t** and a double **l**.

flounder *verb*
> ! Do not confuse **flounder** with **founder. Flounder** means 'stagger clumsily in mud or water' or 'be confused or in difficulty' (*new recruits floundering about in the first week*), whereas **founder** means 'fail or come to nothing' (*the scheme foundered because of lack of backing*).

fluorescent *adjective*
Remember that **fluorescent** and the related word **fluorescence** begin with **fluor-**.

fluoride *noun*
Remember that **fluoride** begins with **fluor-**.

fly *noun and verb*
The different forms of the verb are: **flies**, **flying**; the past tense is **flew** and the past participle is **flown**.

flyer *noun*
Flyer can also be spelled **flier**, with an **i**: both are correct.

focaccia *noun*
Spell **focaccia** with a single **c** and then a double **c**; it is an Italian word.

focus *noun and verb*
The different forms of the verb can be spelled with either a single or a double **s**: **focuses**, **focusing**, **focused** or **focusses**, **focussing**, **focussed**.

The plural of the noun can be spelled either **foci** (as in the original Latin) or **focuses**.

for- *prefix*
See centre pages for words beginning with **for-** and **fore-**.

forbear *verb* (**forbears**, **forbearing**, **forbore**)
❗ Do not confuse **forbear** with **forebear**. **Forbear** means 'stop yourself from doing something' (*he doesn't forbear to write about the bad times*), while **forebear** (which is also sometimes spelled **forbear**) means 'an ancestor' (*our Stone Age forebears*).
RELATED WORD: forbearance *noun*

forbid *verb*
The different forms of this verb are: **forbids**, **forbidding**; the past tense is **forbade** or **forbad** and the past participle is **forbidden**.

forcible *adjective*
Spell **forcible** with **-ible** at the end.

forebear *noun*
❗ **Forebear** (meaning 'an ancestor') can also be spelled **forbear** and is often confused with the verb **forbear** meaning 'stop yourself from doing something'. *See* **FORBEAR**.

forebode *verb*
The beginning of **forebode** should be spelled **fore-**.

foregone *adjective*
Remember that **foregone** (as in *a foregone conclusion*) is spelled with **fore-** at the beginning.

foreign *adjective*
Remember that **foreign** is spelled with the **e** before the **i**; the ending is **-gn**.
RELATED WORD: foreigner *noun*

foreword *noun*
❗ Do not confuse **foreword** with **forward**. *See* **FORWARD**.

forfeit *verb and noun*
Remember that **forfeit** is spelled with the **e** before the **i**.
TIP: you may forf**ei**t your **e**ntire income.

forget *verb* (**forgets**, **forgetting**, **forgot**)
Spell **forget** and the related word **forgetful** with **for-** at the beginning.

forgo *verb*
❗ **Forgo** (meaning 'go without something you want') can also be spelled **forego**, but it is best to use the spelling **forgo** so as to avoid confusion with **forego**, which is an old-fashioned word meaning 'come before'.

format noun and verb

> **RULE:** If a verb ends with a single vowel plus a consonant, and the stress is at the end of the word (as in *refer*), double the last letter when adding **-ing** or **-ed**: formats, **formatting**, **formatted**.

formula noun

The plural of **formula** can be spelled either **formulae** (like the original Latin) for mathematical or scientific senses, or **formulas** for more general senses.

forth adverb

! Do not confuse **forth** with **fourth**. See **FOURTH**.

fortunately adverb

Spell **fortunately** with **-ely** at the end; it is made up of the adjective **fortunate** plus the ending **-ly** in the normal way.

forty noun

Remember that **forty** begins with **for-**.

RELATED WORD: fortieth *adjective*

forum noun

The plural of **forum** is usually spelled **forums**; the plural **fora** (as in the original Latin) is chiefly used when talking about a public square in an ancient Roman city.

forward adverb and adjective

! Do not confuse **forward** with **foreword**. **Forward** mainly means 'towards the front' (*the car moved forward*), whereas **foreword** means 'a short introduction to a book'.

founder verb

! Do not confuse **founder** with **flounder**. See **FLOUNDER**.

fourth adjective

! Do not confuse **fourth** with **forth**. **Fourth** means 'number four in a sequence' (*the fourth and fifth*

centuries), while **forth** means 'away from a starting point' (*the plant put forth new shoots*).

foyer noun

The ending of **foyer** is spelled **-yer**; it is a French word.

fracas noun

Remember that **fracas** ends with **-as**: the **s** is not spoken because it is a French word.

fragrant adjective

The ending of **fragrant** should be spelled **-ant**.

franchise noun and verb

Unlike most verbs ending in **-ise**, **franchise** cannot be spelled with an **-ize** ending. See *centre pages for other verbs that always end in* **-ise**.

free adjective and verb

> **RULE:** Verbs ending in **-oe**, **-ee**, and **-ye** keep the final **-e** when adding **-ing**: frees, **freeing**, **freed**.

freight noun and verb

Remember that **freight** is spelled with the **e** before the **i**.

TIP: the fr**ei**ght train was carrying **e**ngines and **i**mplements.

frequency noun (plural frequencies)

Remember that **frequency** and the related word **frequent** are spelled with **-quen-** in the middle.

fresco noun

The plural of **fresco** (an Italian word) can be spelled either **frescoes** or **frescos**.

fridge noun

Although **fridge** is short for **refrigerator**, it is spelled with a **d** before the **g**.

friend noun

Spell **friend** with **-ie-** in the middle.

frieze *noun*

> **RULE:** **i** before **e** except after **c** (as in *thief*).

frolic *verb and noun*

> **RULE:** If a verb ends in **-ic** (as in *picnic*), add a **k** after the **c** when adding **-ed**, **-ing**, and **-er**: frolics, frolicking, frolicked.

fuchsia *noun*
Remember that **fuchsia** has **-chs-** in the middle: the flower is named after the German botanist Leonhard *Fuchs*.
TIP: fuchsia is a colourful horticultural shrub.

fuel *verb and noun*

> **RULE:** Double the **l** when adding endings which begin with a vowel to words which end in a vowel plus **l** (as in *travel*): fuels, fuelling, fuelled.

fulfil *verb*
Spell **fulfil** with one **l** in the middle and one at the end (the spelling **fulfill** is American).

> **RULE:** Double the **l** when adding endings which begin with a vowel to words which end in a vowel plus **l** (as in *travel*): fulfils, fulfilling, fulfilled.

RELATED WORD: fulfilment *noun*

fullness *noun*
Fullness can also be spelled **fulness**, with a single **l**; both are correct, although **fullness** is far more common.

fulsome *adjective*
Remember that there is only one **l** in **fulsome**.

fungus *noun*
Make the plural of **fungus** by changing the **-us** ending to **-i** (as in the original Latin): **fungi**.

furore *noun*
Remember that **furore** ends with an **e** (the spelling **furor** is American).

fusilli *plural noun*
Remember that **fusilli** has one **s** and a double **l**; it is an Italian word.

f

Gg

g-
The sound *g-* is sometimes spelled *gh-* (as in *ghost*). *If you cannot find the word you are looking for here, check words that begin with **gh-**.*

gaberdine *noun*
Gaberdine can also be spelled **gabardine**: both are correct.

gaiety *noun*
Spell **gaiety** with **-aie-** in the middle (the spelling **gayety** is American).

gallery *noun* (plural **galleries**)
Remember that **gallery** ends with **-ery**.

gallivant *verb*
Spell **gallivant** with a double **l**.

gallop *verb and noun*

RULE: Do not double the final consonant when adding endings which begin with a vowel to a word which ends in a vowel plus a consonant, if the stress is not at the end of the word (as in *target*): **gallops, galloping, galloped**.

gaol *noun and verb*
Gaol can also be spelled **jail**; the spelling **gaol** is only found in British English.

gardener *noun*
The word **gardener** is formed from **garden** plus **-er**, so it is spelled **-ener** at the end.

gargoyle *noun*
Remember that **gargoyle** ends with **-oyle**.

gas *noun and verb*

RULE: Add **-es** to make the plural of words which end in **-s**: **gases** (the spelling **gasses** is mainly American).

RULE: If a one-syllable word ends with a single vowel plus a consonant (as in *stop*), double the last letter when adding **-ing** or **-ed**: **gases** or **gasses**, **gassing**, **gassed**.

gateau *noun*
The plural of **gateau** can be spelled either **gateaux** (like the original French) or **gateaus**.

gauge *noun and verb*
Spell **gauge** with **-au-** in the middle (the spelling **gage** is American).

gazpacho *noun*
Spell **gazpacho** with **gaz-** at the beginning; it is a Spanish word.

generator *noun*
Remember that **generator** ends with **-or**.

generosity *noun*
Spell **generosity** with **-os-** in the middle.

genius *noun* (plural **geniuses**)
Remember that **genius** ends with **-ius**.

ghastly *adjective*
Remember that **ghastly** is spelled with an **h** after the **g**. Other words that begin with **gh-** include *gherkin*, *ghost*, and *ghoul*.

ghetto noun
Spell **ghetto** with **gh-** at the beginning and a double **t**. The plural can be spelled either **ghettos** or **ghettoes**.

gilt adjective
❗ Do not confuse **gilt** with **guilt**. Gilt means 'covered with gold leaf' (*paintings in gilt frames*), whereas **guilt** means 'the fact that someone has done something illegal' (*the prosecution must prove the prisoner's guilt*) or 'a feeling of having done wrong'.

gingham noun
Remember that **gingham** has an **h** after the second **g**.

giraffe noun
Remember that **giraffe** is spelled with one **r** and a double **f**.
TIP: a gi**r**a**ff**e reaching **f**or **f**ruit.

gist noun
Remember that **gist** begins with a **g**.

glamorous adjective

> **RULE:** If a word ends in **-our** (in this case *glamour*), change **-our** to **-or** before adding **-ous**, **-ize**, and some other endings: **glamorous**; **glamorize**.

glamour noun
Remember that **glamour** ends with **-our** (the spelling **glamor** is American).

glimpse verb
Spell **glimpse** with a **p** after the **m**.

glue noun and verb (glues, gluing or glueing, glued)
Gluing is usually spelled without an **e**, although **glueing** is also correct.

gnat noun
Remember that **gnat** begins with **gn-**, although the **g** is not heard when you say the word. Other words that begin with **gn-** include *gnarled*, *gnash*, *gnaw*, *gnome*, and *gnu*.

gnocchi plural noun
Remember that **gnocchi** has a double **c** and an **h** before the **i**; it is an Italian word.

goddess noun
Remember that **goddess** is spelled with a double **d** and a double **s**.

gorilla noun
Remember that **gorilla** is spelled with one **r** and a double **l**.
❗ Do not confuse **gorilla** with **guerrilla**. A **gorilla** is a type of large ape, whereas a **guerrilla** is a member of an independent group fighting against government or other regular forces (*he was held hostage by separatist guerrillas*).

gossamer noun and adjective
Spell **gossamer** with a double **s** and one **m**.

gossip verb and noun

> **RULE:** Do not double the final consonant when adding endings which begin with a vowel to a word which ends in a vowel plus a consonant, if the stress is not at the end of the word (as in *target*): **gossips**, **gossiping**, **gossiped**.

government noun
Remember that **government** is spelled with an **n** before the **m**.
TIP: a gover**n**ment has to gover**n**.

governor noun
The ending of **governor** is spelled **-or**.

graffiti noun
Spell **graffiti** with a double **f** and a single **t**; it is an Italian word.

gram *noun*
Spell **gram** with a single **m** (the spelling **gramme** is rather old-fashioned).

grammar *noun*
Remember that **grammar** is spelled with a double **m**; the ending is **-ar**.

grandad *noun*
Grandad can also be spelled **granddad**, with an extra **d**: both are correct.

granddaughter *noun*
Remember that **granddaughter** is spelled with a double **d**.

grate *verb and noun*
! Do not confuse **grate** with **great**. **Grate** means 'shred food' (*grate the cheese into a bowl*) or 'a metal fireplace frame', whereas **great** means 'very big, important, etc.' (*a great achievement for British science*).

grateful *adjective*
Remember that **grateful** begins with **grate-**.

great *adjective*
! Do not confuse **great** with **grate**. See **GRATE**.

grey *adjective*
Spell **grey** with an **e** in the middle (the spelling **gray** is American).

grief *noun*
RULE: Spell **grief** and the related words **grieve** and **grievance** with **-ie-** in the middle. They all follow the rule **i** before **e** except after **c** (as in *thief*).

grievous *adjective*
RULE: **i** before **e** except after **c** (as in *thief*).

Remember that the ending is spelled **-vous**.

grisly *adjective*
! Do not confuse **grisly** with **grizzly**. **Grisly** means 'causing horror or disgust' (*a grisly crime*), whereas **grizzly** is mainly used to describe a kind of large American bear (*a grizzly bear*) and can also mean 'grey, grey-haired' (*a grizzly beard*).

grotesque *adjective*
Spell **grotesque** with **-esque** at the end.

grotto *noun*
The plural of **grotto** can be spelled either **grottos** or **grottoes**.

grovel *verb*
RULE: Double the **l** when adding endings which begin with a vowel to words which end in a vowel plus **l** (as in *travel*): **grovels, grovelling, grovelled**.

gruelling *adjective*
Spell **gruelling** with a double **l** (the spelling **grueling** is American).

gruesome *adjective*
Remember that **gruesome** is spelled with **-ue-** in the middle.
TIP: he came to a gr**ue**some and **u**npleasant **e**nd.

guacamole *noun*
Remember that **guacamole** begins with **gua-** and ends with **-mole**; it is a Spanish word from Latin America.

guarantee *noun and verb*
RULE: Verbs ending in **-oe**, **-ee**, and **-ye** keep the final **-e** when adding **-ing**: **guarantees, guaranteeing, guaranteed**.

g

guard *noun and verb*
Remember that **guard** and the related word **guardian** begin with **gua-**.

guerrilla *noun*
Guerrilla can also be spelled **guerilla**, with a single **r**; both are correct.
! Do not confuse **guerrilla** with **gorilla**. *See* **GORILLA**.

guess *noun and verb*
Spell **guess** with **-ue-** after the **g** and a double **s** at the end.

guidance *noun*
Remember that **guidance** ends with **-ance**.

guilt *noun*
! Do not confuse **guilt** with **gilt**. *See* **GILT**.
RELATED WORD: guilty *adjective*

guise *noun*
Remember that **guise** begins with **gui-**.

gullible *adjective*
Spell **gullible** with a double **l**; the ending is **-ible**.

gymkhana *noun*
Remember that **gymkhana** is spelled with **-kh-** in the middle.

gymnasium *noun*
The plural of **gymnasium** can be spelled either **gymnasia** (as in the original Latin) or **gymnasiums**.

gynaecology *noun*
Remember that **gynaecology** is spelled **-ae-** in the middle (the spelling **gynecology** is American).

Gypsy *noun* (plural Gypsies)
Gypsy can also be spelled **Gipsy**, with an **i**: both are correct.

Hh

haemorrhage *noun*
Spell **haemorrhage** with a double **r**, then an **h**. Other words that begin with **haem-** (from Greek *haima* 'blood') are *haemophilia* and *haemorrhoid* (the American spellings begin with **hem-**).

hairdryer *noun*
Hairdryer can also be spelled **hairdrier**; both are correct.

halcyon *adjective*
Remember that **halcyon** ends with **-cyon**.

half *noun*

> **RULE:** Change the **-f** to **-ves** to make the plurals of nouns that end in a consonant or a single vowel plus **-f** or **-fe**: *halves*.

hallucinate *verb*
Spell **hallucinate** and the related word **hallucination** with a double **l**.

halo *noun*
The plural of **halo** can be spelled **halos** or **haloes**.

hamster *noun*
Remember that the beginning of **hamster** is spelled **ham-**.

handicap *noun and verb*
Handicap is an exception to the rule that you only double the last letter when adding **-ing** or **-ed** to a word ending in a vowel plus a consonant if the stress is at the *end* of the word. In this case, the stress is at the *beginning* of the word, but you should still double the **p**: *handicaps, handicapping, handicapped*.

handkerchief *noun*
Remember that there is a **d** in **handkerchief**. The plural can be spelled **handkerchiefs** or **handkerchieves**; both are correct.

handsome *adjective*
Remember that there is a **d** in **handsome**.
TIP: a **d**ashing and han**d**some man.

hang *verb* (hangs, hanging, hung or hanged)
Hang has two past tense and past participle forms: **hanged** and **hung**. You should use **hung** in general situations (*they hung out the washing*), while **hanged** should only be used when talking about executing someone by hanging (*the prisoner was hanged*).

happen *verb* (happens, happening, happened)
Spell **happen** with a double **p** and a single **n**.

happy *adjective*

> **RULE:** If an adjective ends in a consonant plus **y**, change the **y** to **i** when adding **-er** or **-est**: *happier, happiest*.

RELATED WORDS: happily *adverb*, happiness *noun*

harangue *verb and noun*

> **RULE:** Drop the final silent **-e** when adding **-ing** or **-ed**: harangues, haranguing, harangued.

harass *verb*
Spell **harass** and the related word **harassment** with a single **r** and a double **s**.

harbour *verb and noun*
Remember that **harbour** ends in **-our** (the spelling **harbor** is American).

hassle *verb*
Spell **hassle** with a double **s** in the middle; the ending is **-le**.

Hawaiian *adjective and noun*
Remember that **Hawaiian** is spelled with a double **i**.

hazard *noun and verb*
Spell **hazard** with a single **z**; the ending is **-ard**.

headdress *noun*
Spell **headdress** with a double **d**.
TIP: a **d**istinctive **d**ecorated hea**dd**ress.

hearse *noun*
Remember that **hearse** begins with **hea-**.

height *noun*
Remember that **height** is spelled with the **e** before the **i**; the ending is **-ght**.

heinous *adjective*
Spell **heinous** with the **e** before the **i**.

heir *noun*
Remember that **heir** begins with an **h**, although it is not heard when you say the word.

helpful *adjective*
Remember that the ending of **helpful** is spelled with a single **l**; it is made up of the word **help** plus the suffix (ending) **-ful**.
RELATED WORD: helpfully *adverb*

heritage *noun*
Remember that **heritage** ends with **-age**.

hero *noun*
The plural of **hero** is made by adding **-es**: heroes.

heroin *noun*
! Do not confuse **heroin** with **heroine**. **Heroin** is an illegal drug, whereas a **heroine** is the main female character in a film, play, or book, or a woman who is admired for her achievements (*she was a true feminist heroine*).

hers *pronoun*
Although **hers** is a possessive pronoun (one that is used to show belonging), it should not be spelled with an apostrophe before the **s**. *See centre pages for more information about apostrophes.*

hesitant *adjective*
The ending of **hesitant** is spelled **-ant**.

heterosexual *adjective and noun*
Remember that **heterosexual** has an **e** between the **t** and the **r**.

hiatus *noun*

> **RULE:** Add **-es** to make the plural of words ending in **-s**: hiatuses.

hiccup *verb and noun*
Hiccup can also be spelled **hiccough**: both are correct.

hideous *adjective*
Remember that **hideous** ends with **-eous**.

hierarchy *noun* (plural hierarchies)
The beginning of **hierarchy** should be spelled **hier-**; the ending is **-archy**.

hijack *verb and noun*
Remember that **hijack** begins with **hi-**.

hilarious *adjective*
Spell **hilarious** with a single **l**.
TIP: we laughed at the hilarious jokes.

hindrance *noun*
Remember that **hindrance**, although related to *hinder*, is spelled **-dr-** in the middle.

hinge *noun and verb* (hinges, hingeing or hinging, hinged)
Hinging is usually spelled without an **e**, although **hingeing** is also correct.

hippo *noun*
The plural of **hippo** is either the same as the singular or is made by adding **-s**: **hippo** or **hippos**.

hippopotamus *noun*
Spell **hippopotamus** with a double **p** before the first **o** and a single **p** after it. The plural can be spelled either **hippopotami** (as in the original Latin) or **hippopotamuses**.

hoard *noun and verb*
❗ Do not confuse **hoard** with **horde**. **Hoard** means 'a secret store of things' (*a hoard of gold*) or 'store things for a period of time', whereas **horde** means 'a large group of people' (*he attracts hordes of female fans*).

hoe *noun and verb*

> **RULE:** Verbs ending in **-oe**, **-ee**, and **-ye** keep the final **-e** when adding **-ing**: hoes, hoeing, hoed.

homeopathy *noun*
Homeopathy and related words such as **homeopathic** can also be spelled **homoeopathy** and **homoeopathic**, with an **o** before the **e**.

homogeneous *adjective*
Remember that **homogeneous** ends with **-eous**.

honorary *adjective*

> **RULE:** If a word ends in **-our** (in this case *honour*), change **-our** to **-or** before adding **-ary**, **-ific**, and some other endings: **honorary**; **honorific**.

honour *noun and verb*
Remember that **honour** ends with **-our** (the spelling **honor** is American).
RELATED WORD: honourable *adjective*

hoof *noun*
The plural of **hoof** can be spelled either **hoofs** or **hooves**: both are correct.

horde *noun*
❗ Do not confuse **horde** with **hoard**. See **HOARD**.

horoscope *noun*
Spell **horoscope** with **horo-** at the beginning.

horrible *adjective*
Spell **horrible** with **-ible** at the end.

horrify *verb* (horrifies, horrifying, horrified)
Remember that the ending of **horrify** is spelled **-ify**. See centre pages for words ending in **-ify** and **-efy**.

hors d'oeuvre *noun*
The plural of **hors d'oeuvre** (a French phrase) can be spelled

h

either **hors d'oeuvre** or **hors d'oeuvres**.

hospitable *adjective*
The ending of **hospitable** is spelled **-able**.

hubbub *noun*
Remember that **hubbub** has a double **b** in the middle and a single **b** at the end.

humiliate *verb*
Spell **humiliate** with a single **m** and a single **l**.

hummus *noun*
Hummus can also be spelled **houmos** or **humous**; it is an Arabic word.

humorous *adjective*

> **RULE:** If a word ends in **-our** (in this case *humour*), change **-our** to **-or** before adding **-ous**, **-ist**, and some other endings: **humorous**; **humorist**.

humour *noun and verb*
Remember that **humour** ends with **-our** (the spelling **humor** is American).

hundred *number*
The ending of **hundred** is spelled **-dred**.

hungry *adjective*

> **RULE:** If a word ends in a consonant plus **-y**, change the **-y** to an **-i** before adding any ending (unless the ending already begins with an **-i**): **hungrier**, **hungriest**.

RELATED WORD: hungrily *adverb*

hurricane *noun*
Spell **hurricane** with a double **r**.

hyacinth *noun*
Spell **hyacinth** with **hya-** at the beginning.

hyena *noun*
Hyena can also be spelled **hyaena**, with an **a** after the **y**: both are correct.

hygiene *noun*

> **RULE:** **i** before **e** except after **c** (as in *thief*).

> **TIP:** good hyg**ie**ne is **e**ssential.
> **RELATED WORD:** hygienic *adjective*

hymn *noun*
Remember that **hymn** has an **n** at the end, although it is not heard when you say the word.

hyphen *noun*
See centre pages for information about using hyphens.

hypochondria *noun*
Remember that **hypochondria** begins with **hypo-** and is spelled **-chon-** in the middle.

hypocrisy *noun*
Remember that **hypocrisy** begins with **hypo-**; the ending is **-isy**.
RELATED WORDS: hypocrite *noun*, hypocritical *adjective*

hypothermia *noun*
Remember that **hypothermia** begins with **hypo-**.

hypothesis *noun*

> **RULE:** Make the plural by changing the **-is** ending to **-es**: **hypotheses**.

-ible
See centre pages for words ending in -ible and -able.

ice *noun and verb*

> **RULE:** Drop the final silent **-e** when adding **-ing** or **-ed**: ices, icing, iced.

RELATED WORD: icy *adjective*

iceberg *noun*
Remember that **iceberg** ends with **-berg**.

ideology *noun* (plural ideologies)
Remember that the beginning of **ideology** is spelled **ideo-**.
RELATED WORD: ideological *adjective*

idiosyncrasy *noun* (plural idiosyncrasies)
Spell **idiosyncrasy** with **-syn-** in the middle; it ends with **-asy**.

idol *noun*
! Do not confuse **idol** with **idle**. **Idol** means 'a person who is admired by many people' (*a pop idol*) or 'a statue or picture of a god that is worshipped', whereas **idle** means 'lazy' or 'pointless' (*idle chatter*).

idyll *noun*
Remember that **idyll** and the related word **idyllic** are spelled with a **y** and then a double **l**.

-ify
See centre pages for words ending in -ify and -efy.

ignorance *noun*
Spell **ignorance** with **-ance** at the end.
RELATED WORD: ignorant *adjective*

illegible *adjective*
Remember that **illegible** is spelled with a double **l**, then **-eg-**; the ending is **-ible**.

illegitimate *adjective*
Spell **illegitimate** with with a double **l**.
RELATED WORD: illegitimacy *noun*

illicit *adjective*
! Do not confuse **illicit** with **elicit**. **Illicit** means 'not allowed by law or rules' (*illicit drugs*), whereas **elicit** means 'draw out a reply or reaction' (*I tried to elicit a smile from Joe*).

illiterate *adjective*
Remember that **illiterate** is spelled with a double **l**.

illusive *adjective*
! Do not confuse **illusive** with **elusive**. See **ELUSIVE**.

imaginary *adjective*
Remember that **imaginary** ends in **-ary**.

imitate *verb*
Spell **imitate** and the related word **imitation** with a single **m**.

immediate *adjective*
Spell **immediate** and the related word **immediacy** with a double **m**.
RELATED WORD: immediately *adverb*

immigrant *noun*
Remember that **immigrant** is spelled with a double **m**; the ending is **-ant**.
RELATED WORD: immigration *noun*

imminent *adjective*
Spell **imminent** with a double **m**; the ending is **-ent**.

immoral *adjective*
Remember that **immoral** is spelled with a double **m**.

impasse *noun*
Remember that **impasse** (a French word) is spelled with **-sse** at the end.

impeccable *adjective*
Spell **impeccable** with a double **c**.

impel *verb*

> **RULE:** Double the **l** when adding endings which begin with a vowel to words which end in a vowel plus **l** (as in *travel*): impels, impelling, impelled.

imperceptible *adjective*
The ending of **imperceptible** is spelled **-ible**.

implement *noun and verb*
Spell **implement** with an **e** in the middle and one at the end.

important *adjective*
The ending of **important** is spelled **-ant**.
RELATED WORD: importance *noun*

impossible *adjective*
Impossible is spelled with **-ible** at the end.

impostor *noun*
Impostor can also be spelled **imposter**: both are correct.

impresario *noun* (plural impresarios)
Remember that **impresario** is spelled with a single **s**.

impression *noun*
Spell **impression** and the related word **impressive** with a double **s**.

improvise *verb*
Unlike most verbs ending in **-ise**, **improvise** cannot be spelled with an **-ize** ending. *See centre pages for other verbs that always end in **-ise**.*

impugn *verb*
Remember that **impugn** is spelled with a **g** before the **n**, although it is not heard when you say the word.

inaccessible *adjective*
Spell **inaccessible** with **-ible** at the end.

inadvertent *adjective*
Remember that **inadvertent** ends with **-ent**.

incandescent *adjective*
The ending of **incandescent** is spelled **-scent**.

incense *verb and noun*
Remember that **incense** ends with **-cense**.

incessant *adjective*
Spell **incessant** with a double **s** in the middle; the ending is **-ant**.

incidentally *adverb*
Remember that **incidentally** ends in **-ally**.

incinerator *noun*
Spell **incinerator** with **-or** at the end.

incise *verb*
Unlike most verbs ending in **-ise**, **incise** cannot be spelled with an **-ize** ending. *See centre pages for other verbs that always end in **-ise**.*
RELATED WORD: incisor *noun*

incommunicado *adjective and adverb*
Remember that **incommunicado** is spelled with a double **m** and a single **n**.

incorrigible *adjective*
Remember that **incorrigible** has a double **r** and ends with **-ible**.

incur *verb*

> **RULE:** If a verb ends with a single vowel plus a consonant, and the stress is at the end of the word (as in *refer*), double the last letter when adding **-ing** or **-ed**: incurs, incurring, incurred.

indebted *adjective*
Remember that **indebted** is spelled with a **b** before the **t**, although it is not heard when you say the word.

indefinite *adjective*
Remember that **indefinite** ends with **-ite**.

indelible *adjective*
Spell **indelible** with **-ible** at the end.

independent *adjective and noun*
Remember that **independent** always ends with **-ent**. *See also* **DEPENDENT**.
TIP: she's an independ**ent** ag**ent**.
RELATED WORD: independence *noun*

indestructible *adjective*
The ending of **indestructible** is spelled **-ible**.

index *verb and noun*
The plural of **index** is usually spelled **indexes**, but can also be spelled **indices** (as in the original Latin) in subjects like science and medicine.

indicator *noun*
Spell **indicator** with **-or** at the end.

indict *verb*
The word **indict** is spelled very differently from the way in which it is said: it ends with **-dict**.

indigenous *adjective*
Remember that **indigenous** is spelled with **-gen-** in the middle.

indiscreet *adjective*
Spell **indiscreet** with **-creet** at the end.

infer *verb*

> **RULE:** If a verb ends with a single vowel plus a consonant, and the stress is at the end of the word (as in *refer*), double the last letter when adding **-ing** or **-ed**: infers, inferring, inferred.

RELATED WORD: inference *noun*

inflammation *noun*
Spell **inflammation** with a double **m**.

infrastructure *noun*
Remember that **infrastructure** begins with **infra-**.

ingenious *adjective*
‼ Do not confuse **ingenious** with **ingenuous**. **Ingenious** means 'clever, original, and inventive' (*an ingenious idea*), whereas **ingenuous** means 'innocent and unsuspecting' (*wide, ingenuous eyes*).

ingredient *noun*
The ending of **ingredient** is spelled **-ient**.

inhabit *verb*

> **RULE:** Do not double the final consonant when adding endings which begin with a vowel to a word which ends in a vowel plus a consonant, if the stress is not at the end of the word (as in *target*): inhabits, inhabiting, inhabited.

inherent *adjective*
Spell **inherent** with -her- in the middle; the ending is -ent.

inheritor *noun*
The ending of **inheritor** is spelled -or.

inhibit *verb*

> **RULE:** Do not double the final consonant when adding endings which begin with a vowel to a word which ends in a vowel plus a consonant, if the stress is not at the end of the word (as in *target*): inhibits, inhibiting, inhibited.

RELATED WORD: inhibition *noun*

initial *noun, adjective, and verb*

> **RULE:** Double the l when adding endings which begin with a vowel to words which end in a vowel plus l (as in *travel*): initials, initialling, initialled.

RELATED WORD: initially *adverb*

initiate *verb*
Remember that **initiate** and the related word **initiation** are spelled with -ti- in the middle.

innate *adjective*
Spell **innate** with a double n.

innocent *adjective and noun*
Remember that **innocent** is spelled with a double n; the ending is -ent.

innovate *verb*
Spell **innovate** and the related word **innovation** with a double n.
TIP: the firm has made a **n**umber of **n**ovel in**n**ovations.

innuendo *noun*
Spell **innuendo** with a double n. The plural can be spelled either **innuendoes** or **innuendos**.

inoculate *verb*
Spell **inoculate** with one n and one c.

input *noun and verb*

> **RULE:** If a verb ends with a single vowel plus a consonant, and the stress is at the end of the word (as in *refer*), double the last letter when adding -ing: inputs, inputting, input.

inquire *verb*
Inquire and the related word **inquiry** can also be spelled **enquire** and **enquiry**. *See* **ENQUIRE**.

insincere *adjective*
Remember that **insincere** ends with -cere.

insistent *adjective*
Spell **insistent** with -ent at the end.

inspector *noun*
The ending of **inspector** is spelled -or.

install *verb*
Spell **install** and the related word **installation** with a double l.

instalment *noun*
Spell **instalment** with one l (the spelling **installment** is American).

> **RULE:** If a word ends in a double l, drop the last l when adding endings which begin with a consonant (here, **install** plus -ment): instalment.

instantaneous *adjective*
Spell **instantaneous** with -eous at the end.

instil *verb*

> **RULE:** Double the l when adding endings which begin with a vowel to words which end in a vowel plus

l (as in *travel*): instils, instilling, instilled.

instructor *noun*
The ending of **instructor** is spelled **-or**.

insure *verb*
! Do not confuse **insure** and **ensure**. *See* **ENSURE**.

intelligent *adjective*
Remember that **intelligent** ends with **-ent**.
RELATED WORD: intelligence *noun*

intelligible *adjective*
The ending of **intelligible** is spelled **-ible**.

intercede *verb*
Spell **intercede** with **-cede** at the end. *See centre pages for other verbs that end in -cede or -ceed.*

interest *noun and verb*
Spell **interest** and the related word **interesting** with **-er-** in the middle.

intermittent *adjective*
Remember that **intermittent** is spelled with a double **t**; the ending is **-ent**.

interrogate *verb*
Spell **interrogate** and the related word **interrogation** with a double **r** and a single **g**.

interrupt *verb*
Spell **interrupt** and the related word **interruption** with a double **r**.
TIP: her speech was interrupted by repeated roars of laughter.

intrigue *verb and noun*
Remember that **intrigue** ends with **-gue**.

introvert *noun and adjective*
The beginning of **introvert** should be spelled **intro-**.

inveigle *verb*
Remember that **inveigle** is spelled with **-ei-** in the middle.

inventor *noun*
Spell **inventor** with **-or** at the end.

invertebrate *noun and adjective*
Spell **invertebrate** with **-teb-** in the middle.

investigator *noun*
The ending of **investigator** is **-or**.

investor *noun*
Remember that **investor** ends with **-or**.

invincible *adjective*
Remember that **invincible** ends with **-ible**.

invisible *adjective*
The ending of **invisible** is spelled **-ible**.

involuntary *adjective*
Spell **involuntary** with **-ary** at the end.

irascible *adjective*
Remember that **irascible** has **-sc-** in the middle; the ending is **-ible**.
TIP: she's irascible, and gets suddenly cross.

irregular *adjective*
Spell **irregular** and the related word **irregularity** with a double **r** at the beginning.

irrelevant *adjective*
Remember that **irrelevant** has a double **r** at the beginning; the ending is **-ant**.

irresistible *adjective*
Spell **irresistible** with a double **r** at the beginning; the ending is **-ible**.

irritable *adjective*
Remember that **irritable** ends with **-able**.

-ise

*See centre pages for verbs ending in
-ise, -ize, and -yse.*

isthmus *noun* (plural isthmuses)
Remember that **isthmus** begins
with **isth-**.

itinerary *noun* (plural itineraries)
Remember that **itinerary** ends with
-erary.

its possessive pronoun
! Do not confuse **its** with **it's**. **Its**
means 'belonging to it' (*turn the
camera on its side*), whereas **it's** is
short for 'it is' (*it's my fault*) or 'it
has' (*it's all gone wrong*).

-ize

*See centre pages for verbs ending in
-ize, -ise, and -yse.*

jacuzzi *noun* (*trademark*)
Spell **jacuzzi** with a single **c** and a double **z**: it is named after its Italian-born American inventor Candido *Jacuzzi*.

jail *verb and noun*
Jail can also be spelled **gaol**: both are correct.

janitor *noun*
The ending of **janitor** is spelled **-or**.

jealous *adjective*
Spell **jealous** and the related word **jealousy** with **jea-** at the beginning.

jeopardize, jeopardise *verb*
Jeopardize and the related word **jeopardy** are spelled with **jeo-** at the beginning.

jewel *noun*
Remember that **jewel** ends in a single **l**. The related words **jewelled**, **jewellery**, and **jeweller** follow the usual rule that you should double the **l** when adding endings which begin with a vowel to words which end in a vowel plus **l** (the spellings **jeweled**, **jewelery**, and **jeweler** are American).

jocular *adjective*
The ending of **jocular** is spelled **-ar**.

jodhpurs *plural noun*
Spell **jodhpurs** with an **h** after the **d**; they are named after the Indian city of *Jodhpur*.
TIP: wear jod**h**purs when riding horses.

jojoba *noun*
Remember that **jojoba** is spelled with two **j**'s: they are spoken like **h**'s because it is a Spanish word.

journey *noun and verb*

> **RULE:** Make the plural of **journey** in the usual way, by adding **-s**: journeys.

jubilee *noun*
Remember that **jubilee** is spelled with a single **l**.

judgement *noun*
Judgement is generally spelled with an **e** after the **g** (the spelling **judgment** is American, although it is also used for British legal matters).

judgemental *adjective*
Judgemental can also be spelled **judgmental**: both are correct, although **judgemental** is more usual in British English.

juggernaut *noun*
Remember that **juggernaut** ends with **-naut**.

jugular *adjective*
The ending of **jugular** is spelled **-ar**.

justify *verb* (**justifies, justifying, justified**)
Remember that the ending of **justify** is spelled **-ify**. *See centre pages for words ending in -ify and -efy*.
RELATED WORD: justifiable *adjective*

Kk

kaftan *noun*
Kaftan can also be spelled **caftan**: both are correct.

kaleidoscope *noun*
Spell **kaleidoscope** with -ei- in the middle.

kangaroo *noun* (plural kangaroos)
Spell **kangaroo** with -gar- in the middle.

karaoke *noun*
Remember that **karaoke** is spelled with an **a** before and after the **r**: it is a Japanese word.

kerb *noun*
! Do not confuse **kerb** with **curb**. See **CURB**.

kernel *noun*
Remember that the ending of **kernel** is spelled -el.

khaki *adjective and noun*
The beginning of **khaki** (a word of Urdu origin) is spelled **kha-**.

kidnap *verb and noun*
Kidnap is an exception to the rule that you only double the last letter when adding endings which begin with a vowel to a word ending in a vowel plus a consonant if the stress is at the end of the word. In this case, the stress is at the *beginning* of the word, but you should still double the **p**: kidnaps, kidnapping, kidnapped.
RELATED WORD: kidnapper *noun*

kilogram *noun*
Kilogram can also be spelled **kilogramme**; both are correct, although **kilogram** is far more common.

kilometre *noun*
Remember that **kilometre** ends with -re (the spelling kilometer is American).

kitsch *noun*
Remember that **kitsch** ends with -sch; it is a German word.

knack *noun*
Remember that **knack** is spelled with a **k** at the beginning, although it is not heard when you say the word. Other words that begin with **kn-** include *knapsack, knead, knee, knickers, knit, knock, knot, know,* and *knuckle.*

knife *noun and verb*

> **RULE:** Change the -fe to -ves to make the plurals of nouns that end in a consonant or a single vowel plus -f or -fe: knives.

knowledge *noun*
Remember that **knowledge** ends with **-edge**.

knowledgeable *adjective*
Knowledgeable can also be spelled **knowledgable**, without the **e** after the **g**: both are correct, although **knowledgeable** is far more common.

Koran *noun*
Koran can also be spelled **Quran** or **Qur'an**: it is an Arabic word meaning 'recitation'.

k

label *noun* and *verb*

> **RULE:** Double the **l** when adding endings which begin with a vowel to words which end in a vowel plus **l** (as in *travel*): **labels**, **labelling**, **labelled**.

laboratory *noun* (plural laboratories)
The ending of **laboratory** is spelled **-ory**.

labour *noun* and *verb*
Remember that **labour** ends with **-our** (the spelling **labor** is American).

labyrinth *noun*
Spell **labyrinth** with **-byr-** in the middle.
TIP: a la**byr**inth of **b**affling **Y**orkshire **r**oads.

lacklustre *adjective*
The ending of **lacklustre** is **-tre** (the spelling **lackluster** is American).

lacy *adjective* (lacier, laciest)
Remember that the ending of **lacy** is spelled **-cy**.

language *noun*
Spell **language** with **-ua-** after the first **g**.

languor *noun*
Remember that **languor** ends with **-uor**.

lapel *noun*
Spell **lapel** with one **p** and one **l**.

larva *noun*
Make the plural of **larva** by adding **-e** (as in Latin): **larvae**.

larynx *noun*
The plural of **larynx** can be spelled either **larynxes** or **larynges** (as in the original Greek).

lasagne *noun*
Remember that **lasagne** ends with **-agne**; it is an Italian word.

lascivious *adjective*
The beginning of **lascivious** is spelled **lasc-**.

laser *noun*
Remember that **laser** is spelled with an **s** and ends with **-er**.

lasso *verb* and *noun*
Remember that **lasso** ends with a single **o**. The plural can be spelled either **lassos** or **lassoes**.

latitude *noun*
Spell **latitude** with two single **t**'s.
TIP: plants from **t**ropical and **t**emperate la**t**i**t**udes.

laugh *verb*
Spell **laugh** with **-augh** after the **l**.
RELATED WORDS: laughable *adjective*, laughter *noun*

launderette *noun*
Launderette can also be spelled **laundrette**, without the first **e**: both are correct.

laureate *noun*
Remember that **laureate** ends with **-eate**.

lavender *noun*
Remember that the ending of **lavender** is **-er**.

lay *verb* (lays, laying, laid)
! Do not confuse **lay** and **lie**. **Lay** means 'put something down' (*they are going to lay the carpet*), whereas **lie** means 'be in a horizontal position to rest' (*why don't you lie down?*). The past tense and past participle of **lay** is **laid** (*they laid the carpet*); the past tense of **lie** is **lay** (*he lay on the floor*) and the past participle is **lain** (*she had lain awake for hours*).

leach *verb*
! Do not confuse **leach** with **leech**. See **LEECH**.

lead *verb* (leads, leading, led)
Remember that the past tense and past participle of **lead** is **led** (*the captain led from the front; she has led a sheltered life*).

leaf *noun*

> **RULE:** Change the **-f** to **-ves** to make the plurals of nouns that end in a consonant or a single vowel plus **-f** or **-fe**: leaves.

league *noun*
Spell **league** with **lea-** at the beginning; the ending is **-ue**.

learn *verb*
Remember that **learn** is spelled with an **a** after the **e**.

lecherous *adjective*
The beginning of **lecherous** is spelled **lech-**.

leech *noun and verb*
! Do not confuse **leech** with **leach**. **Leech** means 'a bloodsucking worm' or 'exploit someone' (*he's leeching off the abilities of others*), whereas **leach** means 'remove a substance from soil by the action of water' (*the nutrient is quickly leached away*).

legendary *adjective*
Remember that **legendary** ends with **-ary**.

legible *adjective*
Spell **legible** with **leg-** at the beginning; the ending is **-ible**.

legionnaire *noun*
Remember that **legionnaire** has a double **n** and that the ending is **-aire**: it is a French word.

legislate *verb*
The beginning of **legislate** is spelled **leg-**.
RELATED WORD: legislator *noun*

legitimate *adjective and verb*
Remember that **legitimate** begins with **leg-** and ends with **-ate**.

leisure *noun*
Remember that **leisure** begins with **leis-**.

length *noun*
The ending of **length** is spelled **-gth**.

lenient *adjective*
Spell **lenient** with **-ent** at the end.

lettuce *noun*
Remember that **lettuce** has a double **t** and that it ends with **-uce**.

leukaemia *noun*
Spell **leukaemia** with **-ae-** in the middle (the spelling **leukemia** is American).

level *noun and verb*

> **RULE:** Double the **l** when adding endings which begin with a vowel to words which end in a vowel plus **l** (as in *travel*): levels, levelling, levelled.

liaise *verb*
Remember that **liaise** is spelled with two **i**'s, one before and one after the **a**.
TIP: you must liaise with colleagues in Italy and Ireland.
RELATED WORD: liaison *noun*

liar *noun*
Remember that **liar** ends with **-ar**.

libel *noun and verb*

> **RULE:** Double the **l** when adding endings which begin with a vowel to words which end in a vowel plus **l** (as in *travel*): libels, libelling, libelled.

RELATED WORD: libellous *adjective*

library *noun* (plural libraries)
Remember that **library** is spelled with two **r**'s, one before and one after the **a**.
RELATED WORD: librarian *noun*

licence *noun*
❗ Do not confuse **licence** with **license**. **Licence** is a noun which means 'a permit to do something' (*a driving licence*), whereas **license** is a verb meaning 'give a permit to someone; allow something' (*the loggers are licensed to cut mahogany trees*). In American English, both the noun and the verb are spelled **license**.

lie *verb*
❗ Do not confuse **lie** with **lay**. *See* **LAY**.
The different verb forms are: lies, lying; the past tense is lay and the past participle is lain.

Liebfraumilch *noun*
Spell **Liebfraumilch** with **Lieb-** at the beginning; it is a German word.

lieutenant *noun*
Lieutenant is spelled very differently from the way in which it is said: it begins with **lieu-**.

life *noun*

> **RULE:** Change the **-fe** to **-ves** to make the plurals of nouns that end in a consonant or a single vowel plus **-f** or **-fe**: lives.

lightning *noun*
❗ Do not confuse **lightning** with **lightening**. **Lightning** means 'a flash of light in the sky caused by electricity' (*thunder and lightning*) or 'very quick', whereas **lightening** is part of the verb **lighten** and means 'getting lighter' (*the sea was lightening from black to grey*).

likeable *adjective*
Likeable can also be spelled **likable**, without the first **e**: both are correct.

likelihood *noun*
Spell **likelihood** with an **i** in the middle.

limit *noun and verb*

> **RULE:** Do not double the final consonant when adding endings which begin with a vowel to a word which ends in a vowel plus a consonant, if the stress is not at the end of the word (as in *target*): limits, limiting, limited.

limousine *noun*
Remember that **limousine** begins with **limou-**: the word comes from *Limousin*, a region of France.

linguine *noun*
Spell **linguine** with **-uine** at the end: it is an Italian word.

liquefy *verb*
Liquefy can also be spelled **liquify**, with an **i** before the **f**: both are correct, but **liquefy** is more common. *See centre pages for words ending in -ify and -efy.*

liqueur *noun*
Spell **liqueur** with two **u**'s, one after the **q** and one before the **r**: it is a French word.

liquor *noun*
Remember that **liquor** ends in **-quor**.

liquorice *noun*
Spell **liquorice** with **-quo-** in the middle (the spelling **licorice** is American).

literary *adjective*
Remember that **literary** ends with **-ary**.

literature *noun*
Spell **literature** with **liter-** at the beginning.

litre *noun*
Remember that **litre** ends with **-re** (the spelling **liter** is American).

liveable *adjective*
Remember that **liveable** is spelled with an **e** in the middle (the spelling **livable** is American).

loaf *noun*

> **RULE:** Change the **-f** to **-ves** to make the plurals of nouns that end in a consonant or a vowel plus **-f** or **-fe**: loaves.

loan *noun and verb*
❗ Do not confuse **loan** with **lone**. **Loan** means 'lend something' (*camcorders will be loaned to select birdwatchers*) or 'something borrowed', whereas **lone** means 'alone; single' (*we sheltered under a lone tree*).

loath *adjective*
loath can also be spelled **loth**, without the **a**: both are correct.
❗ Do not confuse **loath** with **loathe**. **Loath** means 'reluctant to do

something' (*Joe seemed loath to leave*), whereas **loathe** means 'hate someone or something' (*how I loathe that woman!*).
RELATED WORD: loathsome *adjective*

logarithm *noun*
Remember that **logarithm** ends with **-rithm**.

lollipop *noun*
Remember that **lollipop** is spelled with an **i** in the middle.

lone *adjective*
❗ Do not confuse **lone** with **loan**. *See* **LOAN**.

longitude *noun*
Remember that **longitude** is spelled with **-git-** in the middle.

loose *adjective and verb* (looses, loosing, loosed)
❗ Do not confuse **loose** with **lose**. **Loose** means 'not firmly fixed or fastened' (*the handle was loose*) or 'unfasten or set free something', whereas **lose** means 'no longer have something' (*you could easily win or lose £3,000*).

loquacious *adjective*
Remember that **loquacious** ends with **-cious**.

lose *verb* (loses, losing, lost)
❗ Do not confuse **lose** with **loose**. *See* **LOOSE**.

lot *pronoun and noun*
You should spell **a lot** as two words, not one (*a lot can happen in a month*).

louvre *noun*
Remember that **louvre** ends with **-re** (the spelling **louver** is American).

lovable *adjective*
Lovable can also be spelled
loveable, with an **e** after the **v**:
both are correct.

luscious *adjective*
Spell **luscious** with **-sc-** in the
middle.

TIP: lu**sc**ious **s**trawberries and
cream.

lustre *noun*
Remember that **lustre** ends with **-tre**
(the spelling **luster** is American).

luxury *noun* (plural **luxuries**)
Spell **luxury** with **-ury** at the end.

Reference Section

Spelling rules

There are some words, such as *necessary* and *Caribbean*, where you just have to learn the spelling. These kinds of words make up the main part of this book. But there are plenty of other words which follow special rules. Here are some of the main guidelines that you should find helpful in spelling everyday words.

Plurals of Nouns

- Make the plurals of most nouns by simply adding -**s** to the end: *book*, *books*; *journey*, *journeys*.
- If the noun ends with a consonant plus -**y**, make the plural by changing the -**y** to -**ies**: *berry*, *berries*.
- If the noun ends with -**ch**, -**s**, -**sh**, -**x**, or -**z**, add -**es** to make the plural: *church*, *churches*; *bus*, *buses*; *box*, *boxes*.

  But if the -**ch** ending is pronounced -*k*, then just make the plural by adding -**s**: *stomach*, *stomachs*.
- For nouns which end in a consonant or a single vowel plus -**f** or -**fe**, make the plural by changing the -**f** or -**fe** to -**ves**: *half*, *halves*; *knife*, *knives*.
- Nouns which end in two vowels plus -**f** usually form plurals in the normal way, with an -**s**: *chief*, *chiefs*.
- Nouns ending in -**o** can add either -**s** or -**es** in the plural; there is more information about which ending to use in the 'Endings and beginnings' section.
- The plurals of words which have come into English from a foreign language such as Latin or Greek often have two possible spellings: the foreign plural spelling and an English one. For example, the plural of *aquarium* (from Latin) can be spelled *aquaria* (as in Latin) or *aquariums*. If you want to check which is correct, look in the main part of the book.
- Nouns which end in -**is** usually come from Latin; the plurals of these are made by changing the -**is** to -**es**: *crisis*, *crises*; *neurosis*, *neuroses*.

Adding other endings (suffixes)

-ed and -ing

The basic, unchanged part of a verb is called the *infinitive*; it normally occurs with the word 'to', as in 'to *ask*'. To make the form of the verb referring to things that happened in the past (the *past tense*), the ending -**ed** is added to the infinitive (*asked*), and to make the form of the verb referring to things that are still happening (the *present participle*), the ending -**ing** is added (*asking*). Although there is usually no need to make any other changes to the infinitive, there are some cases where spelling changes do occur:

1. If the verb ends with a silent (unspoken) -**e** (as in *bake*), then drop this before -**ed** and -**ing**: *baked*, *baking*. There are some exceptions to this rule:

   ■ verbs ending in -**ee**, -**ye**, and -**oe**, such as *free*, *dye*, and *hoe*, do not drop the final silent -**e** when adding -**ing**: *freeing*, *dyeing*, *hoeing*.

   ■ there are a few verbs (such as *singe*) that keep the final silent -**e** when adding -**ing** (*singeing*) to distinguish them from similar words without the -**e** (such as *sing*).

2. If the verb ends with a vowel plus -**l** (as in *travel*), then double this before -**ed** and -**ing**: *travelled*, *travelling*.

   Note that this rule does not apply in American spelling; for more information, see the 'American spelling' section.

3. If the verb ends with a single vowel plus a consonant, and the stress is at the end of the word (as in *refer*), then double the final consonant before -**ed** and -**ing**: *referred*, *referring*.

4. If the verb ends with a single vowel plus a consonant and the stress is not at the end of the word (as in *target*), do not double the final consonant: *targeted*, *targeting*.

5. If the verb has only one syllable and ends with a single vowel plus a consonant (as in *stop*), then the final consonant should be doubled before -**ed** and -**ing**: *stopped*, *stopping*.

6. If the verb ends with two vowels plus a consonant (as in *treat*), do not double the final consonant: *treated*, *treating*.

7. If the verb ends in -**c** (as in *picnic*), then add a **k** before -**ed**, -**ing**, and -**er**: *picnicked*, *picnicking*, *picnicker*.

Other suffixes beginning with vowels

These include **-able**, **-ion**, **-ous**, **-er**, **-or**, **-ance**, **-ent**, **-ish**, and **-al**. They are generally used to form adjectives and nouns, and their spelling rules are similar to those outlined above for adding **-ed** and **-ing** to verbs.

1. If adding such a suffix to a word that ends with a consonant, the spelling is often straightforward: *adapt, adaptable; addict, addiction; mountain, mountainous; black, blackish.*

2. When adding such a suffix to a word that ends with a final silent **-e**, drop the final **-e**: *inflate, inflation; advise, advisable; dance, dancer.*

3. Keep the final **-e** when adding suffixes to words that end with a soft **-ce** or **-ge** sound: *notice, noticeable; courage, courageous.*

4. When adding these suffixes to verbs ending in a vowel plus **-l**, double the **-l**: *counsel, counsellor; excel, excellent.*

5. Double the final consonant when adding these endings to verbs that end with a single vowel plus a consonant, where the stress is at the end of the word: *refer, referral; begin, beginner.*

6. Do not double the final consonant if the word ends with a single vowel plus a consonant and the stress is not at the end of the word: *visit, visitor; common, commonest.*

7. If the word has only one syllable and ends with a single vowel plus a consonant, double the final consonant: *stop, stopper; dim, dimmest.*

8. Do not double the consonant if the verb ends with two vowels plus a consonant: *sleep, sleeper.*

9. When adding the suffixes **-ous**, **-ious**, **-ary**, **-ation**, **-ific**, **-ize**, and **-ise** to a word which ends in **-our**, you should change the **-our** to **-or** before adding the suffix: *humour, humorous; glamour; glamorize; labour; laborious.*

   Note that the ending should remain as **-our** before other suffixes: *colourful, favourite, odourless.*

Other spelling rules

1. The suffix **-ful** can form nouns or adjectives. It is always spelled with one **l**: *bucketful, scornful, faithful.* The related suffix **-fully** is always spelled with a double **l**: *scornfully, faithfully.*

Spelling rules

2. When adding suffixes to words that end with a consonant plus -**y**, change the final **y** to **i** (unless the suffix already begins with an **i**): *pretty, prettier, prettiest; ready, readily; beauty, beautiful*. This rule also applies when adding the -**s**, -**ed**, and -**ing** endings to verbs ending in -**y**: *defy, defies, defying, defied*.

3. The ending -**ly** is often added to adjectives and nouns to form adverbs and adjectives: *slow, slowly; week, weekly*. If adding -**ly** to an adjective that ends in a consonant plus -**le**, then drop the -**e** and just add -**y**: *gentle, gently; single, singly*.

4. When adding suffixes that begin with a consonant (such as -**ment**, -**ful**, and -**ly**) to words which end in a double **l**, drop the final **l** before adding the ending: *install, instalment; skill, skilful; chill, chilly*.

   The ending -**ness** is an exception to this rule: *small, smallness; ill, illness*.

5. Most people know the rule **i** before **e** except after **c**; this only applies when the sound is *ee*. So you should spell *receive, ceiling*, and *conceive* with -**ei**- because the *ee* sound follows the letter **c**, whereas *piece, believe*, and *thief* are spelled -**ie**- because the *ee* sound does not follow a **c**.

   There are a few exceptions to this rule (such as *seize*), which are given in the main part of the book; you should just learn how to spell these.

6. Always use a capital letter:

   ■ when writing names of people, places, and words relating to them (*Buddha, Buddhism; America, American*)

   ■ at the beginning of a sentence.

   ■ in the titles of books and other publications, films, TV programmes, organizations, special days, etc. (*Pride and Prejudice, the Conservative Party, Christmas*). In such cases, use a capital letter for all the main words but not for words such as 'a', 'an', 'the', 'of,' 'and', etc.

American spelling

The main differences between American and British English spellings are given below:

- British English words that end in -**re** (e.g. *centre, fibre, theatre*) often end in -**er** in American English (*center, fiber, theater*).
- British English words that end in -**our** (e.g. *colour, humour*) usually end with -**or** in American English (*color, humor*).
- Verbs in British English that can be spelled with either -**ize** or -**ise** at the end (e.g. *recognize/recognise*) are always spelled with -**ize** in American English.
- Verbs in British English that end in -**yse** (e.g. *analyse*) are always spelled -**yze** in American English (*analyze*).
- In British spelling, verbs ending in a vowel plus **l** double the **l** when adding endings that begin with a vowel (e.g. *travel, travelled, traveller*). In American English the **l** is not doubled (*travel, traveled, traveler*).
- British English words that are spelled with the double vowels **ae** or **oe** (e.g. *archaeology, manoeuvre*) are just spelled with an **e** in American English (*archeology, maneuver*).
- Some nouns that end with -**ence** in British English (e.g. *licence, defence*) are spelled -**ense** in American English (*license, defense*).
- Some nouns that end with -**ogue** in British English (e.g. *dialogue*) end with -**og** in American English (*dialog*).

Endings and beginnings

Introduction

There are some word endings (suffixes) and beginnings (prefixes) that can be hard to spell because when they are spoken they sound very similar to each other. These include -**able** and -**ible**, **ante**- and **anti**-, and -**ious** and -**eous**. This section gives some helpful tips on how to spell such words and lists the ones which you are most likely to come across.

-able or -ible?

The endings -**able** and -**ible** are found in adjectives that usually mean 'able to be –': for example, *available* ('able to be used or obtained'); *audible* ('able to be heard'). As a general rule, there are far more adjectives ending in -**able** than -**ible**, so you are more likely to be correct if you choose -**able** (but always use a dictionary if you aren't sure). Here are some other tips to help you decide:

■ When a word ends in -**able**, the core part of the word (the part before the ending) is usually a complete English word in itself: for example, *bearable* (from *bear*) or *acceptable* (from *accept*).

■ If the core part of the word ends in a hard *c* (pronounced as in *cab*) or a hard *g* (pronounced as in *go*), then the ending will always be -**able** (as in *amicable* and *navigable*).

■ Here are some of the most common words ending in -**able**:

acceptable	curable	inflatable	peaceable
adaptable	debatable	inimitable	pleasurable
adorable	desirable	justifiable	preferable
advisable	disposable	knowledgeable	readable
amiable	durable	laughable	regrettable
available	eatable	likeable	reliable
bearable	excitable	lovable	saleable
believable	excusable	manageable	serviceable
breakable	fashionable	measurable	sizeable
capable	forgettable	noticeable	suitable
changeable	forgivable	objectionable	tolerable
comfortable	immovable	obtainable	transferable
conceivable	impassable	operable	unmistakable
creatable	impressionable	payable	usable

- When a word ends in -**ible**, it is less likely that the part before the ending is a recognizable English word: for example, in *audible* and *credible*, the words *aud-* and *cred-* do not exist.

- There are some exceptions to this rule: for example, *accessible* and *collapsible* both end in -**ible** even though they are formed from the recognizable words *access* and *collapse* respectively.

- Here are some of the most frequent words ending in -**ible**:

accessible	divisible	illegible	responsible
audible	eligible	incredible	reversible
collapsible	expressible	invincible	suggestible
contemptible	feasible	negligible	susceptible
convertible	flexible	ostensible	tangible
defensible	gullible	permissible	terrible
digestible	horrible	plausible	visible

Nouns ending in -acy and -asy

Of these two endings, the most common is -**acy**. Some of the most familiar nouns with this ending include:

accuracy	conspiracy	intimacy	pharmacy
adequacy	degeneracy	intricacy	piracy
advocacy	delegacy	legacy	primacy
aristocracy	delicacy	legitimacy	privacy
autocracy	democracy	lunacy	profligacy
bureaucracy	diplomacy	literacy	supremacy
candidacy	efficacy	numeracy	surrogacy
celibacy	fallacy	obstinacy	theocracy
confederacy	immediacy	papacy	

There are only four nouns which end in -**asy** and it is best just to remember them: **apostasy, ecstasy, fantasy, idiosyncrasy**.

Words ending in -ance and -ence

The endings -**ance** and -**ence** are both used to make nouns from verbs (such as *performance* from *perform*) or from adjectives (such as *intelligence* from *intelligent*).

Although most of the time you will need to remember these spellings or use a dictionary, here are a few tips and rules to help:

-ance

- If the word is formed from a verb that ends in **-y**, **-ure**, or **-ear**, then the ending will be spelled **-ance**: for example, *alliance* (from *ally*); *endurance* (from *endure*); *appearance* (from *appear*)

- If the part of the word before the ending ends in a hard *c* (as in *cab*) or a hard *g* (as in *go*), then the ending is **-ance**: for example, *elegance*, *significance*. The word *vengeance* is an exception to this rule.

- If the noun is related to a verb ending in **-ate**, then the ending is likely to be **-ance**: for example, *tolerance* (from *tolerate*)

- Here are some of the most common words ending in **-ance**:

abundance	clearance	guidance	provenance
acceptance	compliance	hindrance	relevance
accordance	continuance	ignorance	reliance
acquaintance	contrivance	importance	remembrance
allegiance	conveyance	inheritance	resemblance
alliance	countenance	instance	resistance
allowance	defiance	insurance	significance
appearance	distance	maintenance	substance
appliance	disturbance	nonchalance	surveillance
assistance	dominance	nuisance	sustenance
assurance	elegance	observance	tolerance
attendance	endurance	performance	utterance
balance	fragrance	perserverance	vengeance
circumstance	grievance	protuberance	vigilance

-ence

- If the word is formed from a verb ending in **-ere**, then the ending will be spelled **-ence**: for example, *reverence* (from *revere*); *adherence* (from *adhere*). The word *perseverance* (from *persevere*) is an exception to this rule.

- If the part of the word before the ending ends in a soft *c* (as in *cell*) or a soft *g* (as in *gaol*), then the ending will be **-ence**: for example, *adolescence*, *negligence*

- See the next page for some of the most common words ending in **-ence**:

absence	consequence	incidence	precedence
acquiescence	convenience	indulgence	preference
adherence	correspondence	influence	presence
adolescence	dependence	innocence	prudence
affluence	difference	insistence	recurrence
audience	eloquence	intelligence	reference
benevolence	emergence	interference	residence
circumference	essence	licence	reverence
coherence	evidence	magnificence	sentence
coincidence	excellence	negligence	sequence
competence	existence	obedience	silence
conference	experience	occurrence	transference
confidence	flatulence	patience	vehemence
conscience	impertinence	persistence	violence

Words ending in -ancy/-ency

■ These endings are used to form nouns. The tips given above about **-ance** and **-ence** also generally apply to these words. For example, nouns made from verbs ending in **-y** have the spelling **-ancy** (as in *occupancy* from *occupy*) and nouns with a soft c or a soft g before the ending will be spelled **-ency** (as in *emergency*).

■ Here are some of the most common nouns ending in **-ancy**:

accountancy	discrepancy	infancy	redundancy
ascendancy	expectancy	militancy	tenancy
buoyancy	hesitancy	occupancy	truancy
consultancy	inconstancy	pregnancy	vacancy

■ These are some of the most frequent nouns ending in **-ency**:

agency	currency	fluency	sufficiency
complacency	decency	frequency	tendency
consistency	efficiency	leniency	transparency
constitutency	emergency	proficiency	urgency

Words ending in -ant and -ent

■ These endings are used to form nouns (such as *deodorant* and *adolescent*) or adjectives (such as *arrogant* and *convenient*). Again, similar rules apply to these words as to words ending in **-ance** and **-ence**.

■ Here are some of the most common nouns and adjectives ending in **-ant**:

abundant	consultant	extravagant	observant
accountant	contestant	fragrant	pleasant
applicant	defiant	gallant	radiant
arrogant	deodorant	hesitant	redundant
assistant	deviant	ignorant	relevant
attendant	discordant	important	reluctant
blatant	distant	instant	significant
brilliant	dominant	luxuriant	tolerant
colourant	elegant	militant	triumphant
combatant	expectant	nonchalant	vigilant

■ These are some of the most frequent words ending in **-ent**:

absorbent	different	independent	present
adherent	dissident	innocent	prominent
adolescent	efficient	insolent	prudent
affluent	eloquent	intelligent	recent
ambient	eminent	lenient	recurrent
benevolent	equivalent	magnificent	resident
competent	evident	negligent	reverent
confident	excellent	obedient	silent
consistent	fraudulent	opulent	sufficient
continent	imminent	patient	transient
convenient	impertinent	permanent	turbulent
current	impotent	persistent	urgent
decent	incident	precedent	violent

■ There are a few words that end in **-ant** and **-ent** which need special care. They are both nouns and adjectives (such as *dependant/dependent* and *propellant/propellent*). There are full explanations of these words in the main part of the book.

Note that **independent** is always spelled with **-ent** at the end, whether it is a noun or an adjective.

ante- or anti-?

The best way to remember when to write **ante-** and when to write **anti-** is to make sure you know what the meaning of the word in question is.

■ When the meaning is 'before', use **ante-** (it comes from Latin *ante* in the same sense). It is used to form words such as *antenatal* (before birth) or *anteroom* (a small room leading to a main one).

- There are only a few words beginning with **ante-** meaning 'before' in general use (note that they are not hyphenated):

antebellum	antedate	antenatal
antecedent	antediluvian	antepenultimate
antechamber	antemortem	anteroom

- When the meaning is 'against' or 'preventing', use **anti-** (it comes from Greek *anti* in the same sense). It is used to form words such as *antifreeze* (a substance that prevents water from freezing) or *anti-racism* (the policy of opposing racism).

- **Anti-** words are sometimes hyphenated, especially when the words following **anti-** begin with a vowel (e.g. *anti-aircraft*, *anti-inflammatory*).

- There are far more words beginning with **anti-** than those that begin with **ante-**; some of the most common are:

anti-abortion	anticlockwise	anti-hero	antioxidant
anti-aircraft	anticyclone	antihistamine	antipathy
antibacterial	antidepressant	anti-inflammatory	antiperspirant
antibiotic	antidote	antimalarial	anti-Semitism
antibody	antifreeze	antimatter	antiseptic
anticlimax	antigen	anti-nuclear	antisocial

(**-ary, -ery, or -ory?**)

Knowing which of these endings to choose can be tricky. Here are a few general tips:

-ary

- Words ending in **-ary** can be nouns (*boundary*), adjectives (*ordinary*), or both (*contemporary*).

- They are sometimes related to nouns ending in **-ar**: for example, *burglary* (*burglar*).

- If the part of the word before the ending is not a recognizable English word in itself, then it is often (but not always) the case that the ending will be **-ary** (e.g. *vocabulary*, *library*).

- Here are some of the most common words ending in **-ary**:

adversary	dictionary	library	secretary
anniversary	disciplinary	monetary	solitary
arbitrary	extraordinary	mortuary	stationary
auxiliary	fragmentary	necessary	subsidiary
beneficiary	glossary	obituary	summary
boundary	hereditary	ordinary	temporary
centenary	honorary	parliamentary	tributary
commentary	imaginary	quandary	visionary
complimentary	intermediary	reactionary	voluntary
contemporary	involuntary	revolutionary	vocabulary
contrary	itinerary	rotary	
customary	judiciary	secondary	

-ory

■ Words ending in **-ory** can be nouns (*lavatory*) or adjectives (*derogatory*).

■ They are sometimes related to nouns ending in **-or**: for example, *advisory* (*advisor*).

■ If the part of the word before the ending is not a recognizable English word in itself, then it is often (but not always) the case that the ending will be **-ory** (e.g. *laboratory*, *allegory*).

■ Many words ending in **-ory** are related to English words ending in **-ion**: for example, *introductory* (*introduction*).

■ Here are some of the most common words ending in **-ory**:

accessory	depository	inflammatory	preparatory
advisory	derisory	introductory	priory
allegory	derogatory	inventory	promontory
category	desultory	laboratory	rectory
conciliatory	directory	lavatory	satisfactory
conservatory	dormitory	mandatory	sensory
contradictory	explanatory	memory	signatory
contributory	factory	obligatory	territory
cursory	history	observatory	theory
defamatory	illusory	predatory	victory

-ery

■ Words ending in **-ery** are nearly always nouns (*battery*), and they are often related to words ending in **-er**: for example, *brewery* (*brewer*).

■ The only exceptions to the above are the adjective **slippery** and other adjectives that are based on words that end in **-er** (e.g. *blustery*).

■ If the part of the word before the ending is a recognizable English word in itself, then it is often (but not always) the case that the ending will be **-ery** (e.g. *mockery*). This is also true when the base word ends in an **-e** that is dropped before the **-ery** ending is added (e.g. *brave*; *bravery*) or where it ends in a consonant which is doubled when the ending is added (e.g. *distil*; *distillery*).

■ Here are some of the most common nouns ending in **-ery**:

adultery	celery	gallery	nursery
archery	cemetery	jewellery	pottery
artery	crockery	lottery	recovery
artillery	cutlery	machinery	robbery
bakery	delivery	mastery	scenery
battery	discovery	misery	snobbery
bravery	distillery	mockery	stationery
brewery	flattery	monastery	surgery
butchery	forgery	mystery	trickery

-cede, -ceed, or -sede?

Although there are only ten verbs with these endings in general use, they can cause spelling problems because they are all pronounced with the sound *-seed*. It is best just to learn the correct spellings as shown below.

■ The most common ending is **-cede**:

accede	precede
concede	recede
intercede	secede

■ There are only three words that end with -ceed: **exceed**, **proceed**, and **succeeed**.

■ Only one word ends with -sede: **supersede**.

Words ending in -ch and -tch

The spelling of these words often causes problems; for instance, many people wrongly spell *detach* and *attach* with the ending **-tch**. Here are some simple tips as to which spelling to use:

- If the final -*ch* sound comes after a consonant, the ending is **-ch**: for example, *search*, *church*, *branch*, *finch*.

- When the final -*ch* sound follows a one-letter vowel, it is written **-tch**: for example, *fetch*, *catch*, *pitch*, *watch*, *dispatch*. There are a few exceptions to this rule, listed below:

attach	much	sandwich	which
detach	ostrich	spinach	
enrich	rich	such	

- If the final -*ch* sound comes after a two-letter vowel, the word should be written **-ch**: for example, *teach*, *crouch*, *touch*, *speech*.

Verbs ending in -efy or -ify

Most verbs of this type end with **-ify**. Some of the most familiar include:

amplify	edify	intensify	rectify
beautify	electrify	justify	sanctify
certify	exemplify	modify	signify
clarify	falsify	mystify	simplify
classify	fortify	notify	specify
commodify	gentrify	pacify	terrify
dignify	glorify	purify	testify
disqualify	horrify	qualify	unify
diversify	identify	ratify	verify

There are only four common verbs that end in **-efy**: **liquefy**, **putrefy**, **rarefy**, and **stupefy**. You will sometimes see the spellings **liquify** and **rarify**; these are also correct, but they are far less frequent.

Nouns ending in -er, -or, and -ar

-er

This ending is the most common. It is usually added to verbs to make nouns with the meaning 'a person or thing that does something' (e.g. *builder*, *farmer*, *carrier*, *sprinkler*).

The ending **-er** can also be used to form nouns meaning:

- 'a person or thing having a particular quality or form' (e.g. *double-decker*, *two-wheeler*)

- 'a person belonging to a particular place or group' (e.g. *city-dweller*)
- 'a person concerned with a particular thing' (e.g. *jeweller*)

This group of nouns tend to come from other nouns or adjectives rather than verbs. Here are the most important:

foreigner	mariner	sorcerer
jeweller	milliner	treasurer
lawyer	prisoner	usurer

-or

As with the main use of the ending **-er**, the suffix **-or** is also added to verbs to make nouns meaning 'a person or thing that does something' (e.g. *investigator*, *escalator*).

There are no hard-and-fast rules as to when these nouns are spelled **-or** and when they are written **-er**, but there are fewer such words ending in **-or**. Here are some of the most important:

accelerator	councillor	investigator	projector
actor	counsellor	investor	protector
administrator	decorator	legislator	radiator
auditor	dictator	mediator	refrigerator
calculator	director	narrator	sailor
collector	editor	navigator	spectator
commentator	educator	objector	supervisor
competitor	elevator	operator	surveyor
conductor	escalator	oppressor	survivor
conqueror	governor	orator	translator
conspirator	indicator	perpetrator	vendor
constructor	inspector	processor	ventilator
contractor	inventor	professor	visitor

There is a smaller group of nouns ending in **-or** that do not come from verbs:

ambassador	chancellor	janitor	solicitor
ancestor	creditor	major	sponsor
author	debtor	mayor	successor
aviator	doctor	pastor	suitor
bachelor	emperor	predecessor	tailor
benefactor	equator	proprietor	tenor
captor	impostor	rector	tractor
censor	jailor	senator	victor

Note that there are a few nouns that can be spelled with either **-er** or **-or** (e.g. *adviser/advisor*, *propeller/propellor*). You will find such words given in the main part of the book.

-ar

This ending is used in a few well-known words to mean 'a person who does something' (e.g. *liar*, *beggar*). Note that they are not always related to verbs (e.g. *vicar*, *bursar*).

beggar	bursar	pedlar	scholar
burglar	liar	registrar	vicar

The ending **-ar** is also used in some other nouns:

altar	cellar	guitar	pillar
calendar	collar	hangar	vinegar
caterpillar	dollar	mortar	
cedar	grammar	nectar	

for- or fore-?

To remember when to spell a word with **for-** and when to write **fore-**, think about what the meaning of the word in question is.

- **for-** is added to words to convey the meaning of banning, neglecting, doing without, or giving up: for example, *forbid* (refuse to allow); *forbear* (stop yourself from doing something). It is also sometimes used for emphasis: for example, *forlorn* (very sad or lonely).

- **for-** is much rarer than **fore-** and is not used nowadays to form new words. These are the most common words that begin with **for-**:

forbear	forfeit	forgive	forlorn
forbearance	forget	forgiveness	forsake
forbid	forgetful	forgo	forswear

- Use **fore-** when the meaning is 'before', 'in advance' or 'in front of'. It is used to form words such as *forecourt* (an open area in front of a building) or *forecast* (say what will or may happen in the future).

■ There are far more words beginning with **fore-** than those that begin with **for-**; some of the most common are:

forearm	forefront	forelock	foresight
forebear	foregoing	foreman	foreskin
foreboding	foregone	forename	forestall
forecast	foreground	foreplay	foretaste
foreclose	forehand	forerunner	foretell
forecourt	forehead	foresee	forethought
forefather	foreland	foreshadow	forwarn
forefinger	foreleg	foreshore	foreword

Confusion can arise because some words that begin with **for-** and **fore-** sound the same when spoken and are very similar in appearance. For example, *forbear* means 'stop yourself from doing something', while a *forebear* is an ancestor (and, confusingly, can also be spelled *forbear*). There is more advice on such words in the main part of the book.

-ious or -eous?

Both of these endings are used to form adjectives (e.g. *various*, *hideous*). Words which end with the spelling **-ious** are far more common than those ending in **-eous**, but there are no set rules as to which spelling is correct.

■ Here are some of the most common adjectives ending in **-ious**:

acrimonious	copious	imperious	previous
ambitious	curious	industrious	rebellious
anxious	delicious	ingenious	religious
atrocious	delirious	laborious	serious
audacious	devious	luxurious	studious
capacious	envious	melodious	superstitious
cautious	ferocious	notorious	tedious
ceremonious	glorious	obvious	various
conscious	hilarious	pretentious	victorious

■ Here are the most important adjectives ending in **-eous**:

aqueous	curvaceous	gorgeous	nauseous
beauteous	discourteous	hideous	piteous
bounteous	erroneous	igneous	plenteous
contemporaneous	extraneous	instantaneous	simultaneous
courteous	gaseous	miscellaneous	spontaneous

In addition to the above words, there are a few adjectives which are spelled **-eous** when the different suffix **-ous** is added. This is because the word they are formed from ends in **-ge** and keeps the final **-e** so as to be pronounced with a soft *-ge* sound: for example, *courageous* (from *courage*); *outrageous* (from *outrage*).

Verbs ending in -ise, -ize, or -yse

Many verbs that end in **-ize** can also end in **-ise** (such as *finalize/finalise* or *realize/realise*); both endings are acceptable, although **-ise** is more common in British English. In this dictionary, such verbs are given with the spelling **-ize**, with **-ise** given as an equally correct alternative.

However, there are a smaller number of verbs that must always be spelled with **-ise** at the end. The main reason for this is that **-ise** is not a separate suffix (ending) in such cases, but part of a longer word element, such as **-cise** (meaning 'cutting', as in *excise*), **-mise** (meaning 'sending', as in *compromise*), or **-prise** (meaning 'taking', as in *surprise*).

The most common verbs ending only in **-ise** are given below.

advertise	despise	incise	surmise
advise	devise	prise (meaning	surprise
apprise	disguise	'open')	televise
chastise	excise	promise	
comprise	exercise	revise	
compromise	improvise	supervise	

There are also a few verbs which always end in **-yse** in British English (they are all spelled with the ending **-yze** in American English):

analyse	catalyse	electrolyse	paralyse
breathalyse	dialyse	hydrolyse	psychoanalyse

Plurals of nouns ending in -o

The plurals of most nouns are formed by simply adding **-s** to the end of the word (*bag + s = bags*): the Spelling rules section gives more details about this and the way in which other plurals are formed.

However, there are special rules for nouns that end in **-o**: some nouns ending in **-o** just add **-s** to make the plural, and others add **-es**. You will also see from this and other dictionaries that some plural nouns can be spelled either way. Here are some tips to help you choose the right ending.

■ As a general rule, the majority of nouns ending in **-o** behave in the same way as most other nouns and add **-s** to make the plural (e.g. *solos*, *zeros*), so you are more likely to be correct if you choose **-s** (but check the dictionary if you're not sure)

■ Nouns which end in a vowel (including **y**) before the final o always add **-s** to make the plural: e.g. *studios*, *videos*, *zoos*, *embryos*

■ Here is a list of the most common nouns ending in **-o** that always have **-es** in the plural:

SINGULAR	PLURAL	SINGULAR	PLURAL
buffalo	buffaloes	mosquito	mosquitoes
domino	dominoes	potato	potatoes
echo	echoes	tomato	tomatoes
embargo	embargoes	torpedo	torpedoes
hero	heroes	veto	vetoes

■ Here is a list of the most common nouns that can be spelled with either **-s** or **-es** in the plural:

SINGULAR	PLURAL	SINGULAR	PLURAL
archipelago	archipelagos or archipelagoes	motto	mottos or mottoes
banjo	banjos or banjoes	peccadillo	peccadillos or peccadilloes
cargo	cargos or cargoes	pedalo	pedalos or pedaloes
flamingo	flamingos or flamingoes	portico	porticos or porticoes
		salvo	salvos or salvoes
fresco	frescos or frescoes	tornado	tornados or tornadoes
ghetto	ghettos or ghettoes		
grotto	grottos or grottoes	tuxedo	tuxedos or tuxedoes
halo	halos or haloes	virago	viragos or viragoes
lasso	lassos or lassoes	volcano	volcanos or volcanoes
mango	mangos or mangoes		
memento	mementos or mementoes		

-sion, -tion, or -cion?

These endings form many well-known nouns and people often have problems when writing them. Here are some guidelines to help you choose the correct spelling.

-sion

■ If the ending is pronunced as in *confusion*, then it should be spelled **-sion**. For example:

collision	division	fusion	revision
confusion	erosion	incision	seclusion
decision	explosion	persuasion	vision

■ When the ending comes after an **-l**, it is always spelled **-sion**:

compulsion	emulsion	propulsion	revulsion
convulsion	expulsion	repulsion	

■ When the ending follows an **-n** or **-r**, it is often (but not always) spelled **-sion**. As a general tip, if such a word is related to another one that ends in **-d** or **-se**, then it is likely to be spelled **-sion**: for example, *immersion* (*immerse*); *comprehension* (*comprehend*):

apprehension	comprehension	diversion	immersion
aversion	conversion	extension	version

■ Nouns based on words that end in **-ss**, **-mit**, or **-cede** always end in **-sion**: for example, *permission* (*permit*); *discussion* (*discuss*):

admission	depression	expression	permission
aggression	discussion	impression	submission
commission	emission	obsession	succession

-tion

■ If the ending is pronounced as in *station*, then it should be spelled -**tion**. For example:

addition	duration	nation	solution
ambition	edition	notion	station
caution	emotion	position	vocation

■ If the noun is related to a word ending in -**ate**, then the ending will be -**ation**: for example, *donation* (*donate*):

accommodation	donation	location	rotation
creation	education	mediation	vacation

■ If the ending comes after any consonant apart from -**l**, -**n**, or -**r**, then the ending is spelled -**tion**:

action	connection	infection	reception
affection	deception	interruption	satisfaction
attraction	description	obstruction	suggestion
collection	exception	perception	transaction

■ After -**n** and -**r**, the ending can be -**tion** or -**sion** (see previous page). It is more likely to be -**tion** if the word is related to another one which ends in -**t** or -**tain**: for example, *assertion* (*assert*); *retention* (*retain*):

abortion	assertion	distortion	invention
abstention	detention	exertion	retention

-cion

There are only two common nouns that end in -**cion**: **suspicion**, **coercion**.

Apostrophes

Although many people find it tricky to use apostrophes correctly, the easiest way to get them right is to understand why and when they are used. Apostrophes are used in three ways:

To show belonging

Use an apostrophe to show that a thing or person belongs or relates to someone or something (called the possessive); so instead of saying *the book of Sara* or *the weather of yesterday*, you can write *Sara's book* and *yesterday's weather*.

- with a noun in the singular or most personal names, add an apostrophe plus s: *Sara's book*; *the cat's paws*; *yesterday's weather*

- for personal names that end in -s, add an apostrophe plus s when you would pronounce the resulting form with an extra s: *Charles's house*; *Dickens's novels*; *Thomas's brother*

  Note that there are some exceptions to this rule, especially in names of places, for example: *St Thomas' Hospital*

- for personal names that end in -s but are not spoken with an extra s, just add an apostrophe after the -s: *Bridges' poems*; *Connors' sister*; *Herodotus' writings*

- with a noun in the plural that already ends in -s, add an apostrophe after the -s: *a boys' school*; *two weeks' newspapers*; *the horses' stables*

- with a noun in the plural that does not end in -s, add an apostrophe plus s: *the children's coats*; *men's clothing*

- there are some expressions which contain a double possessive. These are formed with nouns relating to people or with personal names: for example, you can say *she's a friend of Mary's*, using both the possessive word *of* and an apostrophe plus s after *Mary*, or *she's a friend of Mary*, without the apostrophe s – both are correct. The double possessive is not used with nouns referring to an organization: for example, you should say *a friend of the Tate Gallery* not *a friend of the Tate Gallery's*.

- the only case in which you do not need an apostrophe to show belonging is in the group of words called *possessive pronouns*: these are the words *hers*, *its*, *ours*, *theirs*, *yours* (meaning 'belonging to her, it, us, them, or you')

Remember that *its* means 'belonging to it', but *it's* (with an apostrophe) is short for 'it is' or 'it has' (always think what meaning you want before writing these words)

To show that letters or numbers have been omitted

- Use an apostrophe to show that letters have been omitted: for example, *I'm* (short for *I am*); *wasn't* (short for *was not*); *he'll* (short for *he will*); *pick 'n mix* (short for *pick and mix*)
- Use an apostrophe to show that numbers have been omitted, especially in dates: for example, *the winter of '89* (short for *1989*)

To show plurals of letters or numbers

There are some special plurals where an apostrophe should be used, usually so as to make the meaning clear:

- to show the plurals of letters or numbers, use an apostrophe before the s: *there are two p's in appear*; *find all the number 7's*
- use an apostrophe for showing the plurals of some very short words, especially when they end with a vowel: *he was taken aback when the no's overwhelmed the yeses*

You should **not** use an apostrophe for ordinary plurals of nouns such as *pizzas*, *euros*, *cats*, etc. Although in the past people often used to put an apostrophe in plurals of abbreviations such as *MP's*, or in dates made up of numbers such as *1970's*, most people now write them without: *MPs*; *1970s*.

Hyphens

The hyphen is used to link words and parts of words. Although the use of hyphens is quite variable in English, these are the main guidelines on how to use them:

In compound words and phrases

- The hyphen is used to join two or more words so as to form a single word (called a compound word). The hyphen shows that the words have a combined meaning (e.g. *a pick-me-up*) or that there is a relationship between the words that make up the compound: for example, *rock-forming minerals* are minerals that form rocks.

- Use a hyphen when linking the two words of a compound adjective (e.g. *good-hearted, black-haired, right-handed*). When the first part of such compound adjectives is an adverb that does not end in *-ly*, use a hyphen when the compound comes before the noun (*a well-known woman*), but not when the compound comes after the noun (*the woman is well known*).

  Do **not** put a hyphen between an adverb ending in *-ly* and a linked adjective, even when they come before the noun: *a highly competitive market*; *recently published books*.

- Straightforward compounds formed from nouns are now usually spelled either as two words in modern English (e.g. *boiling point, credit card*) or as one (*website, database*). In the past, hyphens were used to avoid a collision of consonants (*ear-ring*), but nowadays such words are usually not hyphenated (*earring*).

- Hyphens are often used to link words to avoid confusion (e.g. *a great-aunt* is not the same as *a great aunt*); this happens especially when a compound expression comes before a noun (e.g. *twenty-odd people came to the meeting* means something very different from *twenty odd people came to the meeting*).

- Verbs made up of more than one word (called *phrasal verbs*), such as *build up* in *continue to build up your pension*, should not be hyphenated. When such a verb is made into a noun, such as *build-up* in a *build-up of traffic*, then you should use a hyphen.

■ Use a hyphen when a compound formed from two nouns is made into a verb (e.g. *a date stamp* but *to date-stamp*).

With prefixes

■ Hyphens can be used to join a prefix ending in a vowel (such as *co-* and *neo-*) to another word, especially if that word begins with a vowel (e.g. *co-opt*, *neo-Impressionism*), although one-word forms are becoming more usual (*cooperate*, *neoclassical*).

■ Use a hyphen to avoid confusion with another word: for example, to distinguish *re-cover* (= provide something with a new cover) from *recover* (= get well again)

In word-breaks

Hyphens can also be used to divide words that are not usually hyphenated for the following reasons:

■ to show where a word is to be divided at the end of a line of writing. Always try to split the word in a sensible place, so that the first part does not mislead the reader: for example, *hel-met* not *he-lmet*; *dis-abled* not *disa-bled*.

■ to stand for a common second element in all but the last word of a list, e.g. *two-*, *three-*, or *fourfold*.

Common misspellings

If you don't know how to spell a word, it can be hard to know where to look for the correct spelling in a dictionary or reference book. The following list gives the top 100 misspellings according to the Oxford English Corpus – an electronic collection of over 2-billion words of real English that helps us to see how the language is being used. The words are arranged in alphabetical order of the incorrect spellings – if you can't find the word you're looking for in the main part of this book, perhaps you can track it down here.

Misspelling	Correct spelling
accomodate, accomodation	accommodate, accommodation (two cs, two ms)
accross	across (one c)
acheive	achieve (i before e)
agressive, agression	aggressive, aggression (two gs)
apparantly	apparently (-ent not -ant)
appearence	appearance (ends with –ance)
arguement	argument (no e after the u)
assasination	assassination (two double s's)
basicly	basically (ends with –ally)
begining	beginning (double n)
beleive, belive	believe (i before e)
bizzare	bizarre (one z)
buisness	business (begins busi-)
calender	calendar (-ar not –er)
Carribean	Caribbean (one r, two bs)
cemetary	cemetery (ends with -ery)
chauffer	chauffeur (ends with -eur)
collegue	colleague (-ea- in the middle)
comming	coming (one m)
commitee	committee (double t)
completly	completely (ends with –ely)
concious	conscious (-sc- in the middle)
curiousity	curiosity (-os- in the middle)
definately	definitely (-ite- not –ate-)
dissapear	disappear (one s, two ps)
dissapoint	disappoint (one s, two ps)

Misspelling	Correct spelling
ecstacy	ecstasy (ends with –sy)
embarass	embarrass (two rs, two s's)
enviroment	environment (n before the m)
existance	existence (ends with –ence)
familar	familiar (ends with –iar)
Farenheit	Fahrenheit (begins with Fahr-)
finaly	finally (two ls)
florescent	fluorescent (begins with fluor-)
foriegn	foreign (e before i)
forseeable	foreseeable (begins with fore-)
fourty	forty (begins with for-)
foward	forward (begins with for-)
freind	friend (i before e)
futher	further (begins with fur-)
gaurd	guard (begins with gua-)
glamourous	glamorous (-mor- in the middle)
goverment	government (n before the m)
happend	happened (ends with –ened)
harrass, harrassment	harass, harassment (one r, two s's)
honourary	honorary (-nor- in the middle)
humourous	humorous (-mor- in the middle)
idiosyncracy	idiosyncrasy (ends with –asy)
immediatly	immediately (ends with –ely)
incidently	incidentally (ends with –ally)
independant	independent (ends with –ent)
interupt	interrupt (two rs)
irresistable	irresistible (ends with –ible)
jist	gist (begins with g-)
knowlege	knowledge (remember the d)
liase, liason	liaise, liaison (remember the second i: liais-)
lollypop	lollipop (i in the middle)
millenium	millennium (two ls, two ns)
miniscule	minuscule (begins with minu-)
Neandertal	Neanderthal (ends with -thal)
neccessary	necessary (one c, two s's)
noticable	noticeable (remember the middle e)
ocassion, occassion	occasion (two cs, one s)
occurance, occurence	occurrence (two cs, two rs)
occured, occuring	occurred, occurring (two cs, two rs)
pavillion	pavilion (one l)
peice	piece (i before e)

Misspelling	Correct spelling
persistant	persistent (ends with -ent)
pharoah	pharaoh (ends with -aoh)
politican	politician (ends with -cian)
Portugese	Portuguese (ends with -guese)
posession	possession (two s's in the middle and two at the end)
prefered, prefering	preferred, preferring (two rs)
propoganda	propaganda (begins with propa-)
publically	publicly (ends with -cly)
realy	really (two ls)
recieve	receive (e before i)
refered, refering	referred, referring (two rs)
religous	religious (ends with -gious)
rember, remeber	remember (-mem- in the middle)
resistence	resistance (ends with -ance)
seige	siege (i before e)
sence	sense (ends with -se)
seperate	separate (-par- in the middle)
succeful	successful (two cs, two s's)
supercede	supersede (ends with -sede)
suprise	surprise (begins with sur-)
tatoo	tattoo (two ts, two os)
tendancy	tendency (ends with -ency)
therefor	therefore (ends with -fore)
threshhold	threshold (one h in the middle)
tommorow, tommorrow	tomorrow (one m, two rs)
tounge	tongue (begins with ton-, ends with -gue)
truely	truly (no e)
unforseen	unforeseen (remember the e after the r)
unfortunatly	unfortunately (ends with -ely)
untill	until (one l at the end)
whereever	wherever (one e in the middle)
wich	which (begins with wh-)
wierd	weird (e before i)

How is English spelling changing?

This book gives you the currently accepted standard spellings of words, and you should always use these. However, the English language is always developing and changing, with alternative spellings constantly arising. We can track these changes through the Oxford English Corpus, which contains all varieties of English, from scientific journals, literary novels, and newspapers, to chat rooms, discussion boards, and blogs. Through the Corpus we can see the emergence of new spellings and forms in informal English (as slang, shorthand, or actual errors) and check for evidence of them being adopted into more standard English.

One of the most interesting examples of spelling change is the adjective *minuscule*. The word derives from a Latin word *minuscula* meaning 'somewhat smaller', but because *minuscule* means 'very small', many people associate it with the word *mini*, and spell it *miniscule* instead. From the Corpus, we've discovered that the spelling *miniscule* now accounts for around 52% of total use, and that this includes examples in creditable printed sources such as newspapers and periodicals as well as in unedited personal blogs. In other words, the non-standard, supposedly 'incorrect' spelling has now overtaken the accepted one in terms of usage.

Although the spelling *miniscule* is slightly more frequent, it has not yet become accepted as standard English and you should still treat it as an error to be avoided: if you go to the entry for *minuscule* in this book, you will see that this is the case. However, what is considered controversial today may become acceptable in the future, and it could be that *miniscule* is added as a valid alternative spelling in a future edition.

The reinterpretation of words like *minuscule*, where a less familiar spelling is changed 'logically' to a more common one, is similar to the process known as *reanalysis*. This is the way in which, over time, people replace an obscure word within a phrase with a similar sounding, more familiar one.

The phrase 'to curry favour' is well known today; but few people realize that the original form of the phrase was 'curry favel'. Here, *curry* means 'to groom or rub down a horse', and *Favel* was a horse in a 14th century French romance, known for his cunning. So 'curry *Favel*' came to mean to use cunning. In time, the name 'Favel' was forgotten, and replaced by the similar-sounding word 'favour', which probably made more sense to later writers than 'Favel'. If such 'errors' make sense, they may be repeated by other writers, and eventually the 'mistake' becomes the accepted form of the phrase.

The Oxford English Corpus allows us to examine this process in action, by comparing the frequency of the old form of a phrase with the frequency of its new form. Here are some examples of phrases that have been changed, with the percentage of examples that each form represents:

Accepted form	%	%	Reanalysis (Changed form)
moot point	97%	3%	mute point
sleight of hand	85%	15%	slight of hand
toe the line	84%	16%	tow the line
fazed by	71%	29%	phased by
home in on	65%	35%	hone in on
a shoo-in	65%	35%	a shoe-in
bated breath	60%	40%	baited breath
free rein	54%	46%	free reign
chaise longue	54%	46%	chaise lounge
buck naked	53%	47%	butt naked
vocal cords	51%	49%	vocal chords
just deserts	42%	58%	just desserts
fount of knowledge/wisdom	41%	59%	font of knowledge/wisdom
strait-laced	34%	66%	straight-laced

At the top of the list, the standard spellings *moot point* and *sleight of hand* are still far more common than the newer *mute point* and *slight of hand*: the changed forms are not well established in the language and are still seen as errors. In the case of *strait-laced* and *straight-laced*, however, the new form is becoming more common than the original, and is now accepted as a valid alternative spelling (as you will see at the entry for *strait-laced* in this book). However, this is the only example to be considered correct, and in general you should always stick to the currently accepted forms. In the meantime, we'll keep track of the ongoing changes through the Corpus – will *strait-laced* disappear from the language completely, or will *tow the line* ever become an acceptable alternative to *toe the line*?

macaroni *plural noun*
Spell **macaroni** with one **c** and one **r**: it is an Italian word.

Machiavellian *adjective*
Remember that **Machiavellian** is spelled with **Machia-** at the beginning; it comes from the name of the Italian statesman Niccolò *Machiavelli*.

mackerel *noun*
The ending of **mackerel** is spelled **-el**.

maelstrom *noun*
Remember that the beginning of **maelstrom** Is spelled **mael-**: it is a Dutch word.

maestro *noun*
The plural of **maestro** can be spelled either **maestros** or **maestri** (as in the original Italian).

magic *noun and verb*

> **RULE:** If a verb ends in **-ic** (as in *picnic*), add a **k** after the **c** when adding **-ed**, **-ing**, and **-er**: magics, magicking, magicked.

> **RELATED WORD:** magical *adjective*

maintenance *noun*
Remember that **maintenance** is spelled with **-ten-** in the middle; the ending is **-ance**.

malign *adjective and verb*
The ending of **malign** is spelled **-ign**.

malodorous *adjective*
Remember that **malodorous** is spelled with **-odor-** in the middle.

manage *verb*
Spell **manage** and the related words **manager** and **management** with an **a** before and after the **n**.

manageable *adjective*

> **RULE:** Keep the final **-e** when adding **-able** to *manage* to make sure that **manageable** is pronounced with a soft *-ge-* sound: manageable.

mango *noun*
The plural of **mango** can be spelled either **mangoes** or **mangos**.

manoeuvre *noun and verb*
Spell **manoeuvre** with **-oeu-** in the middle; the ending is **-re** (the spelling **maneuver** is American).
RELATED WORD: manoeuvrable *adjective*

market *noun and verb*

> **RULE:** If a verb ends with a vowel plus a consonant, and the stress is not at the end of the word (as in *target*), do not double the last letter when adding **-ing** or **-ed**: markets, marketing, marketed.

marmalade *noun*
Remember that **marmalade** begins with **ma-** and also has **-ma-** in the middle.

marriage *noun*

> **RULE:** If a word ends in a consonant plus **-y** (in this case, *marry*), change the **-y** to an **-i** before adding any ending (unless the ending already begins with an **-i**): **marriage**.

martyr *noun and verb*

Remember that **martyr** ends with **-tyr**.

marvel *verb and noun*

> **RULE:** Double the **l** when adding endings which begin with a vowel to words which end in a vowel plus **l** (as in *travel*): **marvels, marvelling, marvelled**.

marvellous *adjective*

Spell **marvellous** with a double **l** (the spelling **marvelous** is American).

masquerade *noun and verb*

Remember that **masquerade** has **-quer-** in the middle.

massacre *noun*

Remember that **massacre** ends with **-cre**.
TIP: the mass**a**cre was a **c**ruel, ruthless **e**xtermination.

matinee *noun*

Matinee can also be spelled **matinée**, with an accent on the first **e** (as in the original French).

matrix *noun*

The plural of **matrix** can be spelled either **matrices** (like the original Latin) or **matrixes**.

mattress *noun*

Spell **mattress** with a double **t** and a double **s**.

maximum *noun*

The plural of **maximum** can be spelled either **maxima** (as in the original Latin) or **maximums**.

mayonnaise *noun*

Spell **mayonnaise** with a double **n**: it is a French word.

meagre *adjective*

Remember that **meagre** ends with **-gre** (the spelling **meager** is American).

meanness *noun*

Spell **meanness** with a double **n** (it is made up of the adjective **mean** plus the ending **-ness**).

medal *noun*

! Do not confuse **medal** with **meddle**. **Medal** means 'a metal disc given as an award' (*a gold medal*), whereas **meddle** means 'interfere' (*don't meddle in people's lives*).

medallist *noun*

Spell **medallist** with a double **l** (the spelling **medalist** is American).

meddle *verb*

! Do not confuse **meddle** with **medal**. *See* **MEDAL**.

medicine *noun*

Spell **medicine** with an **i** after the **d**.
TIP: a medic works in medicine.

medieval *adjective*

Medieval can also be spelled **mediaeval**, with an **a** after the **i**: both are correct.

mediocre *adjective*

Remember that **mediocre** ends with **-cre**.

Mediterranean *noun*

Spell **Mediterranean** with one **d**, one **t** and a double **r**.

m

melodrama *noun*
Remember that **melodrama** and the related word **melodramatic** begin with **melo-**.

memento *noun*
The plural of **memento** can be spelled either **mementos** or **mementoes**.

memorandum *noun*
The plural of **memorandum** can be spelled either **memorandums** or **memoranda** (like the original Latin).

mercenary *adjective and noun*
Remember that **mercenary** ends with **-ary**.

> **RULE:** Make the plural of words that end in a consonant plus **-y** by changing the **-y** to **-ies** (as in *berry/ berries*): mercenaries.

merchandise *noun and verb*
The nouns **merchandise** and **merchandiser** must always be spelled with the ending **-ise**. The verb can also be spelled with the ending **-ize**, although this is far less common than **merchandise**.

meringue *noun*
Remember that **meringue** ends with **-gue**: it is a French word.

merit *noun and verb*

> **RULE:** Do not double the final consonant when adding endings which begin with a vowel to a word which ends in a vowel plus a consonant if the stress is not at the end of the word (as in *target*): merits, meriting, merited.

metallic *adjective*
Spell **metallic** with a double **l**.

metamorphosis *noun*

> **RULE:** Make the plural by changing the **-is** ending to **-es**: metamorphoses.

meteor *noun*
Remember that **meteor** ends with **-eor**.

meteorology *noun*
Spell **meteorology** and the related word **meteorologist** with **-eor-** in the middle.

meter *noun*
! Do not confuse **meter** with **metre**. A **meter** is a device that measures and records something (*a gas meter*), whereas a **metre** is a unit of measurement or the rhythm of a poem. However, the American spelling for both meanings is **meter**.

migraine *noun*
The ending of **migraine** is spelled **-aine**.

mileage *noun*
Remember that **mileage** is spelled with an **e** in the middle.

milieu *noun*
The plural of **milieu** can be spelled either **milieux** (like the original French) or **milieus**.

militate *verb*
! Do not confuse **militate** and **mitigate**. **Militate** means 'be a powerful factor in preventing something' (*laws that militate against personal freedom*), while **mitigate** means 'make something bad less severe' (*drainage schemes helped to mitigate the problem*).

millennium *noun*
Spell **millennium** with a double **l** and a double **n**. The plural can be spelled either **millennia** (like the original Latin) or **millenniums**.

m

RELATED WORD: millennial *adjective*

millimetre *noun*
The ending of **millimetre** is spelled **-re** (the spelling **millimeter** is American).

millionaire *noun*
Spell **millionaire** with a double **l** and a single **n**.
TIP: his lucky lotto numbers made him a millionaire.

mimic *noun and verb*

> **RULE:** If a verb ends in **-ic** (as in *picnic*), add a **k** after the **c** when adding **-ed**, **-ing**, and **-er**: mimics, mimicking, mimicked.

RELATED WORD: mimicry *noun*

minestrone *noun*
The ending of **minestrone** is spelled **-one**; it is an Italian word.

miniature *noun and adjective*
Remember that **miniature** is spelled with an **a** after the second **i**.

minimum *noun and adjective*
The plural of **minimum** can be spelled either **minima** (as in the original Latin) or **minimums**.

ministry *noun* (plural ministries)
The ending of **ministry** is spelled **-try**.

minuscule *adjective*
Remember that **minuscule** is spelled with a **u** after the **n**.

minutiae *plural noun*
The ending of **minutiae** is spelled **-iae**: it is a Latin word.

miscellaneous *adjective*
Remember that **miscellaneous** begins with **misc-** and ends with **-eous**.

mischievous *adjective*

> **RULE:** **i** before **e** except after **c** (as in *thief*).

Remember that **mischievous** ends with **-vous**.
RELATED WORD: mischief *noun*

misdemeanour *noun*
Remember that **misdemeanour** ends with **-our** (the spelling **misdemeanor** is American).

misogynist *noun*
Spell **misogynist** with **-gyn-** in the middle.

misshapen *adjective*
Remember that **misshapen** is spelled with a double **s**.

missile *noun*
Remember that **missile** ends with **-ile**.

misspell *verb*
Spell **misspell** with a double **s**.

The different forms of this verb are: misspells, misspelling; the past tense is misspelt or misspelled.

mitigate *verb*
! Do not confuse **mitigate** and **militate**. *See* **MILITATE**.
RELATED WORD: mitigation

mitre *noun*
Spell **mitre** with **-re** at the end (the spelling **miter** is American).

mnemonic *noun and adjective*
Remember that **mnemonic** is spelled with an **m** before the **n**, although it is not heard when you say the word.
TIP: a mnemonic provides a memorable note.

moccasin *noun*
Spell **moccasin** with a double **c** but a single **s**.

model *noun and verb*

> **RULE:** Double the **l** when adding endings which begin with a vowel to words which end in a vowel plus **l** (as in *travel*): models, modelling, modelled.

molecular *adjective*
Remember that **molecular** ends with **-ar**.

mollusc *noun*
Spell **mollusc** with **-sc** at the end (the spelling **mollusk** is American).

monastery *noun* (monasteries)
The ending of **monastery** is spelled **-ery**.

money *noun*
When used to mean 'sums of money', the plural of **money** is spelled either **moneys** or **monies**.

monologue *noun*
Remember that **monologue** ends with **-logue**.

moreover *adverb*
Remember that **moreover** has an **e** before the **o**.

mortgage *noun and verb*
Remember that **mortgage** is spelled with a **t** after the **r**, although it is not heard when you say the word.

mortuary *noun* (plural mortuaries)
Remember that **mortuary** ends with **-uary**.

mosquito *noun*
The plural of **mosquito** is made by adding **-es**: mosquitoes.

motto *noun*
The plural of **motto** can be spelled either **mottoes** or **mottos**.

mould *noun and verb*
Remember that **mould** and the related word **mouldy** are spelled with a **u** after the **o** (the spellings **mold** and **moldy** are American).

moulder *verb*
Spell **moulder** with **-ou-** in the middle (the spelling **molder** is American).

moult *verb and noun*
Remember that **moult** is spelled with a **u** after the **o** (the spelling **molt** is American).

moussaka *noun*
Spell **moussaka** with a double **s** and a single **k**: it is a Greek word.

moustache *noun*
Remember that **moustache** begins with **mous-** (the spelling **mustache** is American).

movable *adjective*
Movable can also be spelled **moveable**, with an **e** in the middle; both are correct.

mozzarella *noun*
Remember that **mozzarella** is spelled with a double **z**, a single **r** and a double **l**: it is an Italian word.

muesli *noun*
Remember that **muesli** begins with **mues-**; it is a Swiss German word.

municipal *adjective*
Remember that **municipal** ends with **-pal**.

muscle *noun and verb*
❗ Do not confuse **muscle** with **mussel**. **Muscle** means 'the tissue that moves a body part' (*tone up your thigh muscles*), whereas **mussel** means 'a shellfish' (*fish soup with mussels and clams*).

m

RELATED WORD: muscular
adjective

Muslim *noun and adjective*
   Muslim can also be spelled
   Moslem, although **Muslim** is the
   preferred spelling.

mussel *noun*
   ! Do not confuse **mussel** with
   muscle. *See* **MUSCLE**.

mystery *noun* (plural mysteries)
   Remember that **mystery** and the
   related word **mysterious** begin
   with **mys-**.

n-
The sound *n-* is sometimes spelled *gn-* (as in *gnat*), *kn-* (as in *knife*), or *pn-* (as in *pneumatic*). *If you cannot find the word you are looking for here, check words that begin with* **gn-, kn-,** *or* **pn-**.

nacho *noun*

> **RULE:** Make the plural of **nacho** (a Mexican Spanish word) in the usual way, by adding **-s**: **nachos**.

naive *adjective*
Remember that **naive** is spelled with **-ai-** in the middle. It can also be spelled **naïve**, with two dots over the **i**, as in the original French.
TIP: she was na**i**ve, with an **a**ppealing **i**nnocence.
RELATED WORD: naivety *noun*

narcissus *noun*
Spell **narcissus** with **-ciss-** in the middle. The plural can be spelled either **narcissi** (as in Latin) or **narcissuses**.

nausea *noun*
Remember that **nausea** and the related words **nauseous** and **nauseate** begin with **nau-** and have an **e** after the **s**.
TIP: the drug's **s**ide **e**ffects include nau**s**e**a**.

naval *adjective*
! Do not confuse **naval** with **navel**. **Naval** means 'having to do with the navy' (*a naval base*), whereas **navel** means 'the small hollow in a person's belly' (*an outfit slashed to the navel*).

Neanderthal *noun*
Remember that **Neanderthal** begins with a capital **N** and ends with **-thal**.

necessary *adjective*
Remember that **necessary** and the related word **necessity** are spelled with one **c** and a double **s**.
TIP: it's ne**c**e**ss**ary to cut **s**ome **s**ervices.
RELATED WORD: necessarily *adverb*

negligee *noun*
Negligee can also be spelled **négligée** (as in the original French).

negligent *adjective*
The ending of **negligent** is spelled **-ent**.
RELATED WORD: negligence *noun*

negligible *adjective*
Remember that the ending of **negligible** is spelled **-ible**.

negotiate *verb*
Remember that **negotiate** and the related word **negotiation** are spelled with **-tia-** in the middle.

neighbour *noun and verb*
Spell **neighbour** with **neigh-** at the beginning; the ending is **-our** (the spelling **neighbor** is American).

neither *adverb and pronoun*
Remember that **neither** is spelled with the **e** before the **i**.

nerve-racking *adjective*
Nerve-racking can also be spelled **nerve-wracking**, with a **w**: both are correct.

neurosis *noun*

> **RULE:** Make the plural by changing the **-is** ending to **-es**: neuroses.

niece *noun*

> **RULE:** **i** before **e** except after **c** (as in *thief*).

ninety *number*
Spell **ninety** with an **e** between the **n** and the **t**.

ninth *adjective*
Remember that **ninth** begins with **nin-**.

nosy *adjective*
Nosy can also be spelled **nosey**, with an **e**: both are correct.

noticeable *adjective*

> **RULE:** Keep the final **-e** when adding **-able** to *notice* to make sure that **noticeable** is pronounced with a soft *-ce-* sound: noticeable.

nuclear *adjective*
Remember that **nuclear** ends with **-clear**.

nucleus *noun*

> **RULE:** Make the plural by changing the **-us** ending to **-i** (as in Latin): nuclei.

nuisance *noun*
Remember that **nuisance** begins with **nuis-**.

nuptial *adjective*
Remember that **nuptial** ends with **-tial**.

nutrient *noun*
The ending of **nutrient** is spelled **-ent**.

nutritious *adjective*
Remember that **nutritious** ends with **-tious**.

n

Oo

oasis *noun*

> **RULE:** Make the plural by changing the **-is** ending to **-es**: oases.

obedient *adjective*
The ending of **obedient** is spelled **-ent**.
RELATED WORD: obedience *noun*

obituary *noun* (plural obituaries)
Remember that **obituary** ends with **-uary**.

obligatory *adjective*
The ending of **obligatory** is **-ory**.

oblique *adjective*
Remember that **oblique** ends with **-que**.

obscene *adjective*
Spell **obscene** and the related word **obscenity** with **-sc-** in the middle.

obsolete *adjective*
Remember that **obsolete** has an **o** after the **s** as well as one at the beginning.

occasion *noun and verb*
Spell **occasion** with a double **c** and a single **s**.
TIP: a **c**eremony **c**elebrating a **s**pecial o**cc**asion.

occult *noun and adjective*
Spell **occult** with a double **c**.

occupy *verb* (occupies, occupying, occupied)
Spell **occupy** with a double **c**.
RELATED WORD: occupant *noun*

occur *verb*

> **RULE:** If a verb ends with a single vowel plus a consonant, and the stress is at the end of the word (as in *refer*), double the last letter when adding endings which begin with a vowel: occurs, occurring, occurred.

RELATED WORD: occurrence *noun*

ochre *noun*
Spell **ochre** with **-re** at the end (the spelling **ocher** is American).

octagon *noun*
Remember that **octagon** has an **a** after the **t**.

octopus *noun*
Make the plural of **octopus** by adding **-es** (it comes from Greek, so the usual rule for Latin plurals, with the ending **-i**, does not apply): octopuses.

odorous *adjective*

> **RULE:** If a word ends in **-our** (in this case *odour*), change **-our** to **-or** before adding **-ous** and some other endings: odorous.

odour *noun*
Remember that **odour** ends with **-our** (the spelling **odor** is American).

odyssey *noun*
Spell **odyssey** with a double **s**; it comes from the title of a Greek poem describing the adventures of *Odysseus*.

oestrogen *noun*
Remember that **oestrogen** begins with **oe-** (the spelling **estrogen** is American).

oeuvre *noun*
Spell **oeuvre** with **oeu-** at the beginning: it is a French word.

offence *noun*
Remember that **offence** ends with **-ence** (the spelling **offense** is American).

official *adjective and noun*
Spell **official** and the related words **officiate** and **officious** with a double **f**.

omelette *noun*
Remember that **omelette** is spelled with an **e** after the **m** and the ending is **-ette**; it is a French word.

omission *noun*
Spell **omission** with one **m** and a double **s**.
TIP: the book has **m**any **s**erious and **s**ignificant o**miss**ions.
RELATED WORD: omissible *adjective*

omit *verb*

> **RULE:** If a verb ends with a single vowel plus a consonant, and the stress is at the end of the word (as in *refer*), double the last letter when adding **-ing** or **-ed**: omits, omitting, omitted.

omniscient *adjective*
Remember that **omniscient** is spelled with **-sc-** in the middle.

onomatopoeia *noun*
The ending of **onomatopoeia** is spelled **-oeia**; it comes from Greek *onomatopoiia* 'word-making'.

openness *noun*
Remember that **openness** is spelled with a double **n** (it is made

up of the word **open** plus the ending **-ness**).

operate *verb*
Spell **operate** and the related word **operation** with one **p** and one **r**.
RELATED WORD: operator *noun*

operetta *noun*
Spell **operetta** with one **p**, one **r**, and a double **t**.

ophthalmic *adjective*
Ophthalmic and the related words **ophthalmia** and **ophthalmology** are spelled with a **ph** then **th**.

opinion *noun*
Remember that **opinion** is spelled with a single **p**.

opponent *noun*
Spell **opponent** with a double **p** and a single **n**; the ending is **-ent**.

opportunity *noun* (plural opportunities)
Remember that **opportunity** and the related word **opportune** are spelled with a double **p**, followed by **-or-**.

oppose *verb*
Spell **oppose** and the related words **opposite** and **opposition** with a double **p**.

oppress *verb*
Spell **oppress** with a double **p** and a double **s**.

optician *noun*
Remember that **optician** ends with **-cian**.

opus *noun*
The plural of **opus** can be spelled either **opera** (like the original Latin) or **opuses**.

-or
See centre pages for words ending in -or, -ar, and -er.

oral *adjective and noun*
! Do not confuse **oral** with **aural**. **Oral** means 'spoken' or 'having to do with the mouth' (*oral communication skills*), whereas **aural** means 'having to do with the ears or hearing' (*her new album provides pure aural pleasure*).

orbit *noun and verb*

> **RULE:** Do not double the final consonant when adding endings which begin with a vowel to a word which ends in a vowel plus a consonant, if the stress is not at the end of the word (as in *target*): orbits, orbiting, orbited.

original *adjective and noun*
Spell **original** with an **i** before and after the **g**.

ornament *noun*
Remember that **ornament** is spelled with **-nam-** in the middle.

orthopaedic *adjective*
Spell **orthopaedic** with **-pae-** in the middle (the spelling **orthopedic** is American).

-ory
See centre pages for words ending with -ory, -ary, and -ery.

oscillate *verb*
Spell **oscillate** with **osci-** at the beginning, then a double **l**.

ostensible *adjective*
The ending of **ostensible** is spelled **-ible**.

ours *pronoun*
Although **ours** is a possessive pronoun (one that is used to show belonging), it should not be spelled with an apostrophe before the **s**. *See centre pages for more information about apostrophes.*

output *noun and verb*

> **RULE:** If a verb ends with a single vowel plus a consonant, and the stress is at the end of the word (as in *refer*), double the last letter when adding **-ing** or **-ed**: outputs, outputting, output or outputted.

outrageous *adjective*

> **RULE:** Keep the final **-e** when adding **-ous** to *outrage* to make sure that **outrageous** is pronounced with a soft *ge* sound: outrageous.

overrate *verb*
Spell **overrate** with a double **r** (because it is made up of **over-** plus **rate**). Similar words include **overreact**, **overrule**, and **overrun**.

overwhelm *verb*
Remember that **overwhelm** is spelled with an **h** after the **w**.

ox *noun*
The plural of **ox** is **oxen**. It does not follow the usual rule that plurals of words ending in **-x** are made by adding **-es**.

oxygen *noun*
Spell **oxygen** with **oxy-** at the beginning.

Pp

paediatrics *noun*
Remember that **paediatrics**, **paediatrician**, **paedophile**, and other words derived from Greek *pais, paid-* ('child, boy') begin with **paed-** (the spelling **ped-** is American).

paella *noun*
Remember that **paella** begins with **pae-**: it is a Spanish word.

pageant *noun*
The ending of **pageant** is spelled **-eant**.

pail *noun*
! Do not confuse **pail** with **pale**. Pail means 'a bucket', whereas **pale** means 'light in colour' (*pale blue eyes*).

pain *noun and verb*
! **Pain** is often confused with **pane**. **Pain** means 'an unpleasant feeling caused by illness or injury' (*I had agonizing stomach pains*), whereas **pane** means 'a sheet of glass' (*a window pane*).

painful *adjective*
Remember that the ending of **painful** is spelled with a single **l**; it is made up of the word **pain** plus the suffix (ending) **-ful**.
RELATED WORD: painfully *adverb*

pale *adjective*
! Do not confuse **pale** with **pail**. See **PAIL**.

pallet *noun*
! Do not confuse **pallet** with **palate** or **palette**. A **pallet** is 'a platform for moving goods' or 'a makeshift bed'; **palate** means 'the roof of the mouth' or 'a person's ability to distinguish between different flavours' (*flavours that appeal to the American palate*); a **palette** is 'an artist's board for mixing colours'.

pallor *noun*
Remember that **pallor** ends with **-or**.

panache *noun*
Spell **panache** with **-ache** at the end: it is a French word.

pancreas *noun*
The ending of **pancreas** is spelled **-eas**.

pane *noun*
! Do not confuse **pane** with **pain**. See **PAIN**.

panel *noun and verb*

> **RULE:** Double the **l** when adding endings which begin with a vowel to words which end in a vowel plus **l** (as in *travel*): panels, panelling, panelled.

panic *noun and verb*

> **RULE:** If a verb ends in **-ic** (as in *picnic*), add a **k** after the **c** when adding **-ed**, **-ing**, and **-er**: panics, panicking, panicked.

paparazzo *noun*
Spell **paparazzo** with one **r** and a double **z**. Make the plural by

changing the **-o** to **-i** (as in Italian): **paparazzi**.

paradigm *noun*
Remember that the ending of **paradigm** is spelled **-digm**.

paraffin *noun*
Spell **paraffin** with one **r** and a double **f**.

parallel *adjective, noun, and verb*
Spell **parallel** with a double **l** before the **e** and a single **l** after it.

The different forms of the verb are spelled **parallels**, **paralleling**, **paralleled** (it does not follow the usual rule that a final **l** is doubled when adding endings which begin with a vowel to words which end in a vowel plus **l**).

paralyse *verb*
Remember that **paralyse** ends with **-yse** (the spelling **paralyze** is American). *See centre pages for other verbs that end in -yse.*

paraphernalia *noun*
Remember that **paraphernalia** is spelled with **-phern-** in the middle.

parcel *noun and verb*

RULE: Double the **l** when adding endings which begin with a vowel to words which end in a vowel plus **l** (as in *travel*): parcels, parcelling, parcelled.

parenthesis *noun*

RULE: Make the plural by changing the **-is** ending to **-es**: parentheses.

parliament *noun*
Spell **parliament** with **-ia-** before the **m**.
TIP: I **am** a member of parliament.

parlour *noun*
Remember that **parlour** ends with **-our** (the spelling **parlor** is American).

Parmesan *noun*
Spell **Parmesan** with a capital **P** and an **e** after the **m** (it is named after the Italian city of *Parma*).

paroxysm *noun*
Remember that **paroxysm** ends with **-ysm**.

parrot *noun and verb*

RULE: Do not double the final consonant when adding endings which begin with a vowel to a word which ends in a vowel plus a consonant, if the stress is not at the end of the word (as in *target*): parrots, parroting, parroted.

particular *adjective and noun*
The ending of **particular** is spelled **-lar**.
RELATED WORD: particularly *adverb*

passé *adjective*
Passé is a French word and is usually spelled with an accent on the **e**.

passed
! Do not confuse **passed** with **past**. **Passed** is the past tense of the verb **pass** (*I passed Sid on the stairs*), whereas **past** is a preposition meaning 'beyond in time or space' (*we drove past the house; the danger is past*) or an adverb meaning 'so as to go from one side to the other' (*the limousine swept past*).

passenger *noun*
Spell **passenger** with a double **s**, then an **e**.

pastor *noun*
Remember that the ending of **pastor** is spelled **-or**.

p

pâté noun
Pâté is a French word and it should be spelled with an accent (called a circumflex) on the **a** and an acute accent on the **e**.

patient adjective and noun
Remember that **patient** ends with **-ient**.
RELATED WORD: patience noun

patisserie noun
Patisserie has one **t**, a double **s**, and ends with **-ie**: it is a French word.

patrol noun and verb

> **RULE:** Double the **l** when adding endings which begin with a vowel to words which end in a vowel plus **l** (as in *travel*): **patrols, patrolling, patrolled**.

pattern noun and verb
Remember that **pattern** has a double **t**; the ending is **-ern**.

pavilion noun
Spell **pavilion** with a single **l**.

peal noun and verb
❗ Do not confuse **peal** and **peel**. **Peal** means 'ring loudly' (*all the bells began to peal*) or 'a loud ringing sound', whereas **peel** means 'remove the skin from a fruit or vegetable' (*slice and peel two apples*) or 'the skin of a fruit or vegetable'.

peccadillo noun
Spell **peccadillo** with a double **c** and a double **l**. The plural can be spelled either **peccadilloes** or **peccadillos**.

peculiar adjective
Remember that **peculiar** ends with **-iar**.
TIP: he looked at her in a rather peculiar way.

pedal noun and verb (pedals, pedalling, pedalled)
❗ Do not confuse **pedal** with **peddle**. **Pedal** means 'a foot operated lever' or 'make a bicycle move by working the pedals' (*I pedalled along the road*), whereas **peddle** means 'sell goods' (*they peddled their wares in the market*) or 'promote an idea'.

pedestal noun
Remember that **pedestal** has **-des-** in the middle and ends with **-al**.

pedlar noun
Pedlar can also be spelled **peddler**; **peddler** is more common in American English.

peel noun and verb
❗ Do not confuse **peel** with **peal**. *See* **PEAL**.

pejorative adjective
Remember that **pejorative** begins with **pej-**.

pelican noun
Spell **pelican** with a single **l**.

penchant noun
Remember that **penchant** ends in a **t**: the **t** is not spoken because it is a French word.

pencil noun and verb

> **RULE:** Double the **l** when adding endings which begin with a vowel to words which end in a vowel plus **l** (as in *travel*): **pencils, pencilling, pencilled**.

pendant noun and adjective
❗ A **pendant** is a piece of jewellery or a type of light; **pendant** can also be used as an adjective to mean 'hanging down'. The spelling **pendent**, with an **e**, always means 'hanging down' (*pendent catkins*).

penicillin noun
Spell **penicillin** with a double **l**.

peninsula *noun*
❗ Do not confuse **peninsula** and **peninsular**. Peninsula is a noun meaning 'a long, narrow piece of land jutting out into a sea or lake' (*the Florida peninsula*), whereas **peninsular** is an adjective that means 'having to do with a peninsula' (*the peninsular part of Malaysia*).

penitent *adjective and noun*
Remember that **penitent** is spelled with **-nit-** in the middle; the ending is **-ent**.

penne *plural noun*
Spell **penne** with a double **n**; it is an Italian word.

people *plural noun*
Remember that **people** begins with **peo-**; the ending is **-le**.
TIP: some **peo**ple **p**refer **e**ating **o**utdoors.

perceive *verb*
RULE: **i** before **e** except after **c** (as in *receive*).

perceptible *adjective*
Remember that **perceptible** ends with **-ible**.

percolator *noun*
The ending of **percolator** is spelled **-or**.

percussion *noun*
Remember that **percussion** is spelled with a double **s**.

perennial *adjective and noun*
Spell **perennial** with one **r** and a double **n**.

performance *noun*
Remember that **performance** ends with **-ance**.

permanent *adjective*
Remember that **permanent** ends with **-ent**.
RELATED WORD: permanence *noun*

permission *noun*
Spell **permission** with one **m** and a double **s**.
TIP: you **m**ust **s**eek the state's per**miss**ion to live here.
RELATED WORD: permissible *adjective*

permit *verb and noun*
RULE: If a verb ends with a single vowel plus a consonant, and the stress is at the end of the word (as in *refer*), double the last letter when adding **-ing** or **-ed**: permits, permitting, permitted.

pernicious *adjective*
The ending of **pernicious** is spelled **-cious**.

perpendicular *adjective and noun*
Remember that **perpendicular** ends with **-ar**.

perpetrate *verb*
Remember that **perpetrate** and the related word **perpetrator** are spelled **-pet-** in the middle.

persistent *adjective*
The ending of **persistent** is spelled **-ent**.
RELATED WORD: persistence *noun*

personnel *plural noun*
Spell **personnel** with a double **n**; the ending is **-el**.
❗ Do not confuse **personnel** with **personal**. Personnel means 'workers in an organization or members of the armed forces' (*there's a lack of qualified personnel*), whereas **personal** means 'having to do with or owned by a person' (*personal belongings*).

P

persuade *verb*
Spell **persuade** and the related words **persuasion** and **persuasive** with **-sua-** in the middle.

petulant *adjective*
Remember that **petulant** ends with **-ant**.

pharaoh *noun*
Remember that **pharaoh** ends with **-aoh**.

pharmacy *noun* (plural **pharmacies**)
Spell **pharmacy** and the related words **pharmaceutical** and **pharmacist** with an **a** after the **m**.

phenomenon *noun*
Make the plural of **phenomenon** by changing the **-on** ending to **-a** (as in the original Greek): **phenomena**.

phlegm *noun*
Remember that **phlegm** is spelled with a **g** before the **m**, although it is not heard when you say the word.

phoenix *noun*
The beginning of **phoenix** is spelled **phoe-**.

piccalilli *noun*
Spell **piccalilli** with a double **c**, a single **l**, and then a double **l**.

picnic *noun and verb*

> **RULE:** If a verb ends in **-ic**, add a **k** after the **c** when adding **-ed**, **-ing**, and **-er**: **picnics, picnicking, picnicked**.

> **RELATED WORD:** **picnicker** *noun*

piece *noun and verb*

> **RULE:** **i** before **e** except after **c** (as in *thief*).

pigeon *noun*
Remember that **pigeon** is spelled **-ge-** in the middle.

pilaf *noun*
Pilaf is a Turkish word, and can also be spelled **pilaff** or **pilau**.

pimiento *noun*
Pimiento (a Spanish word) can also be spelled **pimento**, without the **i** in the middle.

> **RULE:** Make the plural in the usual way, by adding **-s**: **pimientos**.

piranha *noun*
Remember that **piranha** ends with **-ha**: it is a Portuguese word.

pirouette *noun and verb*
Spell **pirouette** with **-ou-** in the middle and **-ette** at the end: it is a French word.

pistachio *noun* (plural **pistachios**)
Remember that **pistachio** is spelled with **-ach-** in the middle.

piteous *adjective*
The ending of **piteous** is spelled **-eous**.

pitta *noun*
Pitta can also be spelled **pita**, but this spelling is most often found in American English.

pizzeria *noun*
Remember that **pizzeria** has an **e** after the double **z** (although it is related to *pizza*): it is an Italian word.

plagiarize, plagiarise *verb*
Spell **plagiarize** and the related words **plagiarism** and **plagiarist** with **-gia-** in the middle.

plague *noun and verb*

> **RULE:** Drop the final silent **-e** when adding **-ing** or **-ed**: **plagues, plaguing, plagued**.

plateau *noun and verb* (plateaus, plateauing, plateaued)
The plural of the noun can be spelled either **plateaux** (as in the original French) or **plateaus**.

plausible *adjective*
The ending of **plausible** is spelled **-ible**.

playwright *noun*
Remember that the ending of **playwright** is spelled **-wright** (from the old-fashioned word **wright** meaning 'a maker or builder').

please *verb*
Remember that **please** and the related words **pleasant** and **pleasure** begin with **plea-**.

plebeian *noun and adjective*
Spell **plebeian** with **-eian** at the end.

plough *noun and verb*
Remember that the ending of **plough** is spelled **-ough** (the spelling **plow** is American).

plummet *verb* (plummets, plummeting, plummeted)
Spell **plummet** with a double **m** and a single **t**.

pneumatic *adjective*
Remember that **pneumatic** is spelled with **pneu-** at the beginning (it is from Greek *pneuma* 'wind').

pneumonia *noun*
Spell **pneumonia** with **pneu-** at the beginning (it is from Greek *pneumon* 'lung').

poignant *adjective*
Remember that **poignant** is spelled with **-gn-** in the middle; the ending is **-ant**.

pole *noun*
❗ Do not confuse **pole** with **poll**. **Pole** means 'a long, thin piece of metal or wood' or 'a point at the opposite end to another' (*she and Tom were poles apart in temperament*), whereas **poll** means 'the process of voting in an election' (*voters go to the polls next week*) or 'record someone's vote or opinion'.

politician *noun*
The ending of **politician** is spelled **-cian**.

pollution *noun*
Spell **pollution** and the related words **pollute** and **pollutant** with a double **l**.

poltergeist *noun*
Remember that **poltergeist** ends with **-geist**: it is a German word.

pompous *adjective*
Remember that **pompous** ends with **-ous**.
RELATED WORD: pomposity *noun*

poppadom *noun*
Poppadom (a Tamil word) can also be spelled **poppadum** or **popadom**: all are correct.

porcelain *noun*
Remember that **porcelain** ends with **-ain**.

pore *verb and noun*
❗ Do not confuse **pore** with **pour**. **Pore** means 'study or read closely' (*I spent hours poring over cookery books*) or 'a tiny opening in the skin', whereas **pour** means 'flow in a steady stream' (*water poured off the stones*).

porridge *noun*
Remember that **porridge** ends with **-idge**.

p

portico *noun*
The plural of **portico** can be spelled either **porticoes** or **porticos**.

Portuguese *adjective and noun*
Remember that **Portuguese** is spelled with **-ue-** after the **g**.
TIP: she welcomed her Portu**gue**se **gue**sts.

possess *verb*
Spell **possess** and the related words **possession** and **possessive** with a double **s** before and after the **e**.
RELATED WORD: possessor *noun*

possible *adjective*
The ending of **possible** is spelled **-ible**.
RELATED WORD: possibility *noun*

potato *noun*
The plural of **potato** is made by adding **-es**: potatoes.

pour *verb*
❗ Do not confuse **pour** with **pore**. *See* **PORE**.

practice *noun*
❗ Do not confuse **practice** with **practise**. **Practice** is a noun meaning 'the action of doing something rather than the theories about it' (*putting policy into practice*), whereas **practise** is a verb meaning 'do something repeatedly to improve your skill' (*they were practising for the Olympics*). In American English, both the noun and the verb are spelled **practice**.

practitioner *noun*
Remember that **practitioner** is spelled with **-tit-** in the middle.

prairie *noun*
Spell **prairie** with an **i** after the **a**.

pre- *prefix*
Words which begin with **pre-** followed by another word which begins with an **e** (such as *pre-*

eminent, *pre-empt*, and *pre-existing*) are usually spelled with a hyphen. *See centre pages for more information about hyphens.*

precede *verb*
Remember that **precede** ends with **-cede**. *See centre pages for other verbs that end in **-cede** or **-ceed**.*
RELATED WORD: precedent *noun*

precis *noun*
Precis is a French word and can also be spelled **précis**, with an accent on the **e**: the **s** is not spoken.

preconceived *adjective*

> **RULE: i** before **e**, except after **c** (as in *receive*).

precursor *noun*
The ending of **precursor** is spelled **-or**.

predator *noun*
The ending of **predator** is spelled **-or**.

predecessor *noun*
Remember that **predecessor** is spelled with a double **s** and ends with **-or**.

prefer *verb*

> **RULE:** If a verb ends with a single vowel plus a consonant, and the stress is at the end of the word (as in *refer*), double the last letter when adding **-ing** or **-ed**: prefers, preferring, preferred.

RELATED WORDS: preferable *adjective*, preference *noun*

prejudice *noun and verb*
Remember that **prejudice** begins with **prej-**.

preparation *noun*
Spell **preparation** with **-ar-** in the middle.

p

prerogative *noun*
Remember that **prerogative**
begins with **pre-**.
TIP: the **pre**rogative **p**owers and
rights **e**njoyed by the monarch.

prescribe *verb*
! Do not confuse **prescribe** with
proscribe. **Prescribe** means
'recommend a medicine' (*the
doctor prescribed antibiotics*) or
'state officially that something
should be done' (*a customs union
prescribed by the Treaty of Rome*),
whereas **proscribe** means 'officially
forbid something' (*gambling was
strictly proscribed by the authorities*).

presence *noun*
Remember that **presence** ends
with **-ence**.
RELATED WORD: present *adjective*

presumptuous *adjective*
Remember that **presumptuous** is
spelled with a **p** after the **m**; the
ending is **-uous**.

pretence *noun*
The ending of **pretence** is spelled
-ce (the spelling **pretense** is
American).

priest *noun*

RULE: i before **e** except after **c** (as
in *thief*).

primeval *adjective*
Primeval can also be spelled
primaeval, with an **a** before the **e**:
both are correct.

principal *adjective and noun*
! Do not confuse **principal** with
principle. **Principal** means 'main or
most important' (*the country's
principal cities*), whereas **principle**
means 'a law, rule, or theory that
something is based on' (*the general
principles of law*).

prise *verb*
! Do not confuse **prise** with **prize**.
Prise means 'force something
apart or open' (*he prised open a
bottle of beer*), whereas **prize**
means 'a reward for an
achievement' or 'value something
very highly' (*Africa's cultural
treasures are prized by collectors*). In
American English, the spelling
prize is used for both words.

privilege *noun and verb*
Remember that **privilege** ends
with **-ege**.

procedure *noun*
Spell **procedure** with **-ced-** in the
middle.

proceed *verb*
Remember that **proceed** ends with
-ceed. *See centre pages for other
verbs that end in* **-cede** *or* **-ceed**.

process *noun and verb*
Spell **process** and the related word
processor with one **c** and a double
s.

prodigal *adjective and noun*
Remember that **prodigal** ends with
-al.

profession *noun*
Spell **profession** with one **f** and a
double **s**.

professor *noun*
Remember that **professor** has one
f and a double **s**; the ending is **-or**.

profit *noun and verb*

RULE: Do not double the final
consonant when adding endings
which begin with a vowel to a
word which ends in a vowel plus a
consonant, if the stress is not at
the end of the word (as in *target*):
profits, profiting, profited.

RELATED WORD: profitable
adjective

p

prognosis noun

> **RULE:** Make the plural by changing the **-is** ending to **-es**: prognoses.

programme noun and verb
Remember that **programme** ends with **-amme**, unless it is used in computing senses, when **program** is correct. In American English, it is always spelled **program**.

projector noun
Remember that the ending of **projector** is spelled **-or**.

prologue noun
Remember that **prologue** ends with **-logue** (the spelling **prolog** is American).

prominent adjective
The ending of **prominent** is spelled **-ent**.
RELATED WORD: prominence noun

promise noun and verb
Unlike most verbs ending in **-ise**, **promise** cannot be spelled with an **-ize** ending. *See centre pages for other verbs that always end in -ise.*

pronunciation noun
Remember that, although it is related to *pronounce*, **pronunciation** is spelled with **-nun-** in the middle.

propaganda noun
Remember that **propaganda** has an **a** after the second **p**.

propagate verb
Spell **propagate** and the related word **propagation** with an **a** after the second **p**.

propel verb

> **RULE:** Double the **l** when adding endings which begin with a vowel to words which end in a vowel plus **l** (as in *travel*): propels, propelling, propelled.

propellant noun
As a noun, **propellant** is always spelled with the ending **-ant**.

propellent adjective
As an adjective, **propellent** is usually spelled with the ending **-ent**, although **propellant** is also correct.

propeller noun
Propeller can also be spelled **propellor**: both are correct, but **propeller** is much more common.

prophesy verb
❗ Do not confuse **prophesy** with **prophecy. Prophesy** is a verb meaning 'say that something will happen in the future' (*the media prophesied that he would resign at the weekend*), whereas **prophecy** is a noun meaning 'a prediction about what will happen' (*a bleak prophecy of war*).

proponent noun
Remember that **proponent** ends with **-ent**.

proprietor noun
Remember that **proprietor** ends with **-or**.

proscribe verb
❗ Do not confuse **proscribe** with **prescribe**. *See* **PRESCRIBE**.

prosecute verb
Remember that **prosecute** and the related word **prosecutor** begin with **prose-**.

prostate noun
❗ Do not confuse **prostate** with **prostrate. Prostate** means 'a gland surrounding the bladder of male mammals', whereas **prostrate** means 'lying face downwards' (*he fell prostrate on the ground*) or 'throw oneself flat on the ground'.

protector
Remember that **protector** ends with **-or**.

p

protégé *noun*
> **Protégé** and the feminine form **protégée** are French words and are usually spelled with an accent on the first and second **e**'s.

protein *noun*
> Remember that **protein** is spelled with the **e** before the **i**: it does not follow the rule of **i** before **e** except after **c**.
> **TIP:** it is **e**ssential to **i**nclude prot**ei**n in your diet.

protuberance *noun*
> Remember that **protuberance** is spelled with **-tube-** in the middle.

Provençal *adjective and noun*
> **Provençal** is a French word and is usually written with an accent (called a cedilla) below the **c**.

psalm *noun*
> Remember that **psalm** begins with **ps-**, although the **p** is not heard when you say the word. Other words that begin with **ps-** include *pseudonym*, *psoriasis*, and the words such as *psyche* shown below.

psyche *noun*
> **Psyche** is one of a group of words that come from Greek *psukhē* 'life, breath, soul'. Other words that begin with **psych-** include *psychedelic*, *psychology*, and *psychiatrist*.

psychoanalyse *verb*
> Remember that **psychoanalyse** ends with **-lyse** (the spelling **psychoanalyze** is American). *See centre pages for other verbs that end in -yse.*

psychosis *noun*
> **RULE:** Make the plural of **psychosis** by changing the **-is** ending to **-es**: *psychoses*.

pterodactyl *noun*
> Remember that **pterodactyl** begins with a **p-**, although it is not heard when you say the word.

publicly *adverb*
> Remember that **publicly** is made up of the word **public** and the ending **-ly**. It is an exception to the rule that you add **-ally** (rather than **-ly**) when making adjectives that end in **-ic** into adverbs.

puerile *adjective*
> Remember that **puerile** is spelled with an **e** after the **u**.

punctilious *adjective*
> Remember that **punctilious** is spelled with a single **l**.

puncture *noun and verb*
> Spell **puncture** with a **c** in the middle.

Punjabi *noun and adjective*
> **Punjabi** can also be spelled **Panjabi**, with an **a**; both are correct but **Punjabi** is more common.

punnet *noun*
> Spell **punnet** with a double **n**.

pupa *noun*
> Make the plural of **pupa** by adding **-e** (as in Latin): **pupae**.

purchase *noun and verb*
> Remember that **purchase** ends with **-ase**.

purée *noun and verb* (purées, puréeing, puréed)
> **Purée** is a French word and it is usually spelled with an accent on the first **e**, although **puree** is also correct.

p

pursue *verb*
Remember that **pursue** begins with
pur-.

putrefy *verb*
Remember that **putrefy** ends with
-efy. *See centre pages for words
ending in -ify and -efy.*

pygmy *noun* (plural **pygmies**)
Pygmy can also be spelled **pigmy**;
both are correct.

pyjamas *plural noun*
Remember that **pyjamas** begins
with **py-** (the spelling **pajamas** is
American).

pyrrhic *adjective*
Spell **pyrrhic** with a double **r**; the
ending is **-hic**. The word comes
from *Pyrrhus*, a king of Epirus in
ancient Greece, whose victory over
the Romans cost very heavy losses.

p

quadruped *noun*
Remember that **quadruped** has a **u** following the **r**.

quandary *noun* (plural quandaries)
The ending of **quandary** is spelled **-dary**.

quantitative *adjective*
Remember that **quantitative** is spelled with **-tat-** before the ending **-ive**.

quarrel *noun and verb*

> **RULE:** Double the **l** when adding endings which begin with a vowel to words which end in a vowel plus **l** (as in *travel*): quarrels, quarrelling, quarrelled.

querulous *adjective*
Remember that **querulous** has three **u**'s: one after the **q**, one in the middle, and one at the end.

query *noun and verb*

> **RULE:** If a word ends in a consonant plus **-y** (as in *defy*), change the **-y** to an **-i** before adding any ending (unless the ending already begins with an **-i**): queries, querying, queried.

questionnaire *noun*
Remember that **questionnaire** (a French word) is spelled with a double **n** and ends with **-aire**.

queue *noun and verb* (queues, queuing or queueing, queued)
Queuing is usually spelled without an **e** before the **i**, although **queueing** is also correct.
! Do not confuse **queue** with **cue**. See **CUE**.

quiescent *adjective*
Spell **quiescent** and the related word **quiescence** with **-sc-** in the middle.

quite *adverb*
! Do not confuse **quite** with **quiet**. **Quite** means 'completely' (*are you quite certain?*) or 'moderately' (*it's quite warm outside*), whereas **quiet** means 'making little or no noise' (*she spoke in a quiet voice*).

quixotic *adjective*
Spell **quixotic** with an **x** before the **o**. The word comes from Don *Quixote*, hero of a book by the Spanish writer Cervantes.

quiz *noun and verb*

> **RULE:** If a one-syllable word ends with a single vowel plus a consonant (as in *stop*), double the last letter when adding endings which begin with a vowel: quizzes, quizzing, quizzed.

> **RELATED WORD:** quizzical *adjective*

Quran *noun*
Quran (or **Qur'an**) are alternative ways of spelling **Koran**.

r-

The sound *r-* is sometimes spelled *wr-* (as in *wreck*). *If you cannot find the word you are looking for here, check words that begin with* **wr-**.

rabbit *noun and verb* (rabbits, rabbiting, rabbited)

Spell **rabbit** with a double **b** and one **t**.

racism *noun*

Remember that **racism** and the related word **racist** begin with **rac-**.

rack *noun and verb*

‼ The words **rack** and **wrack** are often confused. When used as a noun, **rack** is always spelled with an **r** (*a magazine rack*). The verb can be spelled **rack** or **wrack**, but only when it means 'cause great pain to someone' (*he was racked/wracked with guilt*): the meanings 'put something in a rack' or 'accumulate something' should always be spelled **rack** (*she racked up high telephone bills*). In the phrase *rack and ruin*, both **rack** and **wrack** are acceptable.

racket *noun*

Racket can also be spelled **racquet** when it means 'a bat used in tennis, squash, or badminton'.

raconteur *noun*

Remember that **raconteur** ends with **-eur**: it is a French word.

radiator *noun*

Remember that **radiator** ends with **-or**.

radicchio *noun*

Spell **radicchio** with a double **c**, then an **h**; it is an Italian word.

radio *noun and verb*

> **RULE:** Make the plural of **radio** in the usual way, by adding **-s**: radios.

The verb forms are: radioes, radioing, radioed.

radius *noun*

The plural of **radius** can be spelled either **radii** (as in the original Latin) or **radiuses**.

ragout *noun*

Remember that **ragout** ends in a **t**: the **t** is not spoken because it is a French word.

rampant *adjective*

The ending of **rampant** is spelled **-ant**.

rancour *noun*

Remember that **rancour** ends with **-our** (the spelling **rancor** is American).

ransom *noun and verb*

The ending of **ransom** is spelled **-om**.

rapport *noun*

Remember that **rapport** is spelled with a double **p** and ends with a **t**: the **t** is not spoken because it is a French word.

rarefy *verb*

Rarefy can also be spelled **rarify**, with an **i** in the middle, although

rarefy is much more common. *See centre pages for words ending in -ify and -efy.*

rarity *noun* (plural **rarities**)
Remember that, although it is related to *rare*, **rarity** is spelled with an **i** in the middle.

raspberry *noun* (plural **raspberries**)
Remember that **raspberry** has a **p** before the **b**.
TIP: ras**p**berry sauce with **p**eaches and **b**ananas.

ratatouille *noun*
Spell **ratatouille** (a French word) with **-oui-** in the middle; the ending is **-lle**.

rateable *adjective*
Rateable can also be spelled **ratable**, without the first **e**: both are correct.

ratio *noun*

RULE: Make the plural of **ratio** in the usual way, by adding **-s**: **ratios**.

ravioli *plural noun*
Spell **ravioli** with a single **v** and a single **l**: it is an Italian word.

razor *noun and verb*
The ending of **razor** is spelled **-or**.

re- *prefix*
Words which begin with **re-** are usually spelled without a hyphen (*react*). However, if the word to which **re-** is linked begins with an **e**, then a hyphen is used to make it clear (*re-enter*). *See centre pages for more information about hyphens.*

reactionary *adjective and noun* (plural **reactionaries**)
The ending of **reactionary** is spelled **-ary**.

reactor *noun*
Remember that the ending of **reactor** is spelled **-or**.

ready *adjective and verb* (**readies, readying, readied**)

RULE: If a word ends in a consonant plus **-y**, change the **-y** to an **-i** before adding any ending (unless the ending already begins with an **-i**): **readier, readiest**.

RELATED WORD: **readiness** *noun*

really *adverb*
Remember that **really** is spelled with a double **l**.

reassess *verb*
Remember that **reassess** and the related word **reassessment** are spelled with a double **s**, then another double **s**.

rebel *noun and verb*

RULE: Double the **l** when adding endings which begin with a vowel to words which end in a vowel plus **l** (as in *travel*): **rebels, rebelling, rebelled**.

RELATED WORDS: **rebellion** *noun*, **rebellious** *adjective*

recede *verb*
Remember that **recede** ends with **-cede**. *See centre pages for other verbs that end in -cede or -ceed.*

receipt *noun*

RULE: **i** before **e** except after **c** (as in *receive*).

Remember that **receipt** has a silent **p** before the **t**.

receive *verb*

RULE: **i** before **e** except after **c**.

r

recess *noun and verb*
Spell **recess** with a single **c** and a double **s**.

recognize, recognise *verb*
Remember that **recognize** and the related word **recognition** are spelled with -cog- in the middle.
RELATED WORD: recognizable *adjective*

recommend *verb*
Spell **recommend** and the related word **recommendation** with a single **c** and a double **m**.
TIP: he re**c**o**mm**ended that I **c**ut out **m**ilk and **m**eat from my diet.

reconnaissance *noun*
Spell **reconnaissance** with a double **n** and a double **s**; the ending is -ance.

reconnoitre *verb*
Remember that there is a double **n** in **reconnoitre**; the ending is -re (the spelling **reconnoiter** is American).

recruit *verb and noun*
The ending of **recruit** is spelled -uit.

rector *noun*
The ending of **rector** is spelled -or.

recur *verb*

> **RULE:** If a verb ends with a single vowel plus a consonant, and the stress is at the end of the word (as in *refer*), double the last letter when adding endings which begin with a vowel: recurs, recurring, recurred.

RELATED WORD: recurrence *noun*

reducible *adjective*
Remember that **reducible** ends with -ible.

redundant *adjective*
The ending of **redundant** is spelled -ant.

re-elect *verb*
Spell **re-elect** with a hyphen after the first **e**. Other words beginning with **re-** that have a hyphen are *re-educate, re-emerge, re-enact, re-enter,* and *re-examine. For more information, see* **RE-.**

refectory *noun* (plural refectories)
Remember that **refectory** ends with -ory.

refer *verb*

> **RULE:** If a verb ends with a single vowel plus a consonant, and the stress is at the end of the word, double the last letter when adding endings which begin with a vowel: refers, referring, referred.

RELATED WORDS: reference *noun*, referral *noun*

referendum *noun*
The plural of **referendum** can be spelled either **referenda** (like the original Latin) or **referendums**.

reflector *noun*
The ending of **reflector** is spelled -or.

refrigerate *verb*
Spell **refrigerate** and the related word **refrigerator** with -frig- in the middle.

regime *noun*
Regime can also be spelled **régime**, with an accent on the first **e** (as in the original French).

registrar *noun*
Remember that **registrar** ends with -trar.
RELATED WORD: registry *noun*

regret *verb*

> **RULE:** If a verb ends with a single vowel plus a consonant, and the stress is at the end of the word (as in *refer*), double the last letter when adding endings which begin with a vowel: regrets, regretting, regretted.

RELATED WORD: regrettable *adjective*

regulator *noun*
Remember that the ending of **regulator** is spelled **-or**.

rehearse *verb*
Remember that **rehearse** and the related word **rehearsal** are spelled with **-ear-** in the middle.

reign *verb and noun*
! Do not confuse **reign** with **rein**. **Reign** means 'rule as king or queen' (*Queen Elizabeth reigns over the UK*) or 'the period of a king's or queen's rule', whereas **rein** means 'the strap used to control a horse,' or 'control something' (*she reined back her impatience*).

rein *noun and verb*
! Do not confuse **rein** with **reign**. The correct phrase is **a free rein** (from the original meaning of using reins to control a horse).

relevant *adjective*
Remember that **relevant** ends with **-ant**.

reliance *noun*
Spell **reliance** with **-ance** at the end.
RELATED WORD: reliant *adjective*

relieve *verb*

> **RULE:** **i** before **e** except after **c** (as in *thief*).

RELATED WORD: relief *noun*

religious *adjective*
Remember that **religious** is spelled with **-ious** at the end.
RELATED WORD: religion *noun*

reluctant *adjective*
The ending of **reluctant** is spelled **-ant**.
RELATED WORD: reluctance *noun*

remember *verb*
Spell **remember** with **-em-** then another **-em-**.
RELATED WORD: remembrance *noun*

reminisce *verb*
Remember that **reminisce** ends with **-sce**.
RELATED WORD: reminiscent *adjective*

remission *noun*
Spell **remission** with one **m** and a double **s**.

remit *verb and noun*

> **RULE:** If a verb ends with a single vowel plus a consonant, and the stress is at the end of the word (as in *refer*), double the last letter when adding endings which begin with a vowel: remits, remitting, remitted.

RELATED WORD: remittance *noun*

remnant *noun*
Remember that **remnant** ends with **-ant**.

renaissance *noun*
Spell **renaissance** with a single **n** and a double **s**: it is a French word.

rendezvous *noun and verb*
(rendezvouses, rendezvousing, rendezvoused)
Rendezvous is a French word; the plural of the noun is also spelled **rendezvous**.

r

renunciation *noun*
Remember that, although it is related to *renounce*, **renunciation** is spelled **-nun-** in the middle.

reoccur *verb*

RULE: If a verb ends with a single vowel plus a consonant, and the stress is at the end of the word (as in *refer*), double the last letter when adding endings which begin with a vowel: reoccurs, reoccurring, reoccurred.

RELATED WORD: reoccurrence *noun*

repel *verb*

RULE: Double the **l** when adding endings which begin with a vowel to words which end in a vowel plus **l** (as in *travel*): repels, repelling, repelled.

repellent *adjective and noun*
Repellent can also be spelled **repellant**; both spellings are acceptable, although **repellent** is far more common.

repertoire *noun*
Remember that **repertoire** has an **r** before the **t** and ends in **-oire**: it is a French word.

repetition *noun*
Spell **repetition** and the related word **repetitive** with **-pet-** then **-it-** in the middle.

reply *verb and noun*

RULE: If a word ends in a consonant plus **-y** (as in *defy*), change the **-y** to an **-i** before adding any ending (unless the ending already begins with an **-i**): replies, replying, replied.

repossess *verb*
Spell **repossess** and the related word **repossession** with a double **s**, then another double **s**.

reprehensible *adjective*
The ending of **reprehensible** is spelled **-ible**.

representative *adjective*
Remember that **representative** has **-tat-** before the ending **-ive**.

reprieve *verb and noun*

RULE: **i** before **e** except after **c** (as in *thief*).

reprise *noun and verb*
Unlike most verbs ending in **-ise**, **reprise** cannot be spelled with an **-ize** ending. *See centre pages for other verbs that always end in -ise.*

resemblance *noun*
The ending of **resemblance** is spelled **-ance**.

reservoir *noun*
Remember that **reservoir** is spelled with an **r** before the **v**.
TIP: a reservoir of rainwater in the valley.

resident *noun*
The ending of **resident** is spelled **-ent**.
RELATED WORD: residence *noun*

resilient *adjective*
Remember that **resilient** only has one **l**; the ending is **-ent**.

resistance *noun*
The ending of **resistance** is spelled **-ance**.
RELATED WORDS: resistant *adjective*, resistor *noun*

resonant *adjective*
The ending of **resonant** is spelled **-ant**.

respirator *noun*
Remember that **respirator** ends with **-or**.
RELATED WORD: respiratory *adjective*

response *noun*
The ending of **response** is spelled **-se**.

responsible *adjective*
The ending of **responsible** is spelled **-ible**.
RELATED WORD: responsibility *noun*

restaurant *noun*
Remember that **restaurant** is spelled with **-au-** between the **t** and **r**: it is a French word.

restaurateur *noun*
Although **restaurateur** (a French word) is related to *restaurant*, it is not spelled with an **n** before the second **t**.

résumé *noun*
! **Résumé** means 'a summary' (*a quick résumé of events*); it is a French word, and is usually spelled with accents on the **e**'s. It should not be confused with **resume**, which means 'begin again after a pause' (*the talks will resume in April*).

resurrect *verb*
Spell **resurrect** and the related word **resurrection** with a single **s** and a double **r**.

resuscitate *verb*
Remember that **resuscitate** is spelled with **-susc-** in the middle.

retaliate *verb*
There is only one **l** in **retaliate** and the related word **retaliation**.

retardant *adjective and noun*
The ending of **retardant** is spelled **-ant**.

reticent *adjective*
Remember that **reticent** ends with **-cent**.

retrieve *verb*

> **RULE: i** before **e**, except after **c** (as in *thief*).

RELATED WORD: retrieval *noun*

revel *verb and noun*

> **RULE:** Double the **l** when adding endings which begin with a vowel to words which end in a vowel plus **l** (as in *travel*): revels, revelling, revelled.

RELATED WORD: reveller *noun*

reverent *adjective*
The ending of **reverent** is spelled **-ent**.

reversible *adjective*
Remember that the ending of **reversible** is spelled **-ible**.

revise *verb*
Unlike most verbs ending in **-ise**, **revise** cannot be spelled with an **-ize** ending. *See centre pages for other verbs that always end in **-ise**.*

revolutionary *adjective and noun* (plural revolutionaries)
The ending of **revolutionary** is spelled **-ary**.

rhapsody *noun* (plural rhapsodies)
Remember that **rhapsody** begins with **rha-**

rhinoceros *noun*
Spell **rhinoceros** with **rh-** at the beginning; the ending is **-ceros**. The plural is **rhinoceros** or **rhinoceroses**.

rhododendron *noun*
Remember that **rhododendron** begins with **rhodo-** and ends with **-on**.

r

rhombus noun
The plural of **rhombus** can be spelled either **rhombuses** or **rhombi** (like the original Latin).

rhubarb noun
The beginning of **rhubarb** is spelled **rhu-**.

rhyme noun and verb
Remember that **rhyme** begins with **rhy-**.

rhythm noun
Remember that **rhythm** is spelled with **rhy-** at the beginning, then **-thm**.
TIP: rhythm really has **y**our **t**wo **h**ips **m**oving.

ricochet verb and noun
Spell **ricochet** with **-chet** at the end: the **t** is not spoken because it is a French word.

ricotta noun
Spell **ricotta** with one **c** and a double **t**: it is an Italian word.

ridiculous adjective
Remember that the beginning of **ridiculous** is spelled **rid-**; the ending is **-ulous**.

Riesling noun
The beginning of **Riesling** (a German word) is spelled with the **i** before the **e**.

righteous adjective
The ending of **righteous** is spelled **-eous**.

rigorous adjective

RULE: If a word ends in **-our** (in this case *rigour*), change **-our** to **-or** before adding **-ous** and some other endings: **rigorous**.

rigour noun
Remember that **rigour** ends with **-our** (the spelling **rigor** is American).

ring noun and verb
❗ Do not confuse **ring** with **wring**. *See* **WRING**.
The different forms of the verb are: **rings**, **ringing**; the past tense is **rang** and the past participle is **rung**.

riposte noun
Spell **riposte** with **ri-** at the beginning; it ends with an **e**.

risotto noun (plural risottos)
Spell **risotto** with one **s** and a double **t**: it is an Italian word.

risqué adjective
Risqué is a French word and is usually spelled with an accent on the **e**.

rival noun and verb

RULE: Double the **l** when adding endings which begin with a vowel to words which end in a vowel plus **l** (as in *travel*): **rivals**, **rivalling**, **rivalled**.

RELATED WORD: rivalry noun

rivet noun and verb

RULE: Do not double the final consonant when adding endings which begin with a vowel to a word which ends in a vowel plus a consonant, if the stress is not at the end of the word (as in *target*): **rivets**, **riveting**, **riveted**.

rococo adjective
Spell **rococo** with two single **c**'s.

role noun
❗ Do not confuse **role** with **roll**. **Role** means 'a part played by an actor' (*he was known for TV roles*), whereas **roll** mainly means 'move by turning

over and over' or 'a rolling movement' (*a roll of the dice*).

roof *noun and verb*
The most usual plural of **roof** is **roofs**, although **rooves** is sometimes used.

rosé *noun*
Rosé is a French word and should be written with an accent on the **e**.

Rottweiler *noun*
Remember that **Rottweiler** is spelled with a double **t** and a single **l** (the dog is named after the German town of *Rottweil*).

rouble *noun*
Rouble can also be spelled **ruble**: both are correct.

route *noun and verb* (routes, routeing or routing, routed)
Routing is usually spelled without an **e**, although **routeing** is also correct.

rudimentary *adjective*
The ending of **rudimentary** is spelled **-ary**.

rue *verb* (rues, rueing or ruing, rued)
Rueing can also be spelled **ruing**: both are correct.

rumbustious *adjective*
The ending of **rumbustious** is spelled **-tious**.

rumour *noun and verb*
Remember that **rumour** ends with **-our** (the spelling **rumor** is American).

r

Ss

s-
The sound *s-* is sometimes spelled *ps-* (as in *psalm*). *If you cannot find the word you are looking for here, check words that begin with **ps-**.*

sabotage *verb and noun*
Spell **sabotage** with one **b** and one **t**: it is a French word.
RELATED WORD: saboteur *noun*

saccharin *noun and adjective*
Saccharin is spelled without an **e** when it is used as a noun meaning 'an artificial sweetener', but it should be spelled with an **e** when used as an adjective meaning 'too sentimental' (*saccharine music*).

sachet *noun*
Remember that **sachet** ends in **-et**: the **t** is not spoken because it is a French word.

sacrifice *noun*
Remember that **sacrifice** and the related word **sacrificial** have an **i** after the **r**.

sacrilege *noun*
Spell **sacrilege** with an **i** after the **r**; the ending is **-lege**.
RELATED WORD: sacrilegious *adjective*

safety *noun*
Spell **safety** with an **e** between the **f** and the **t**.

Sagittarius *noun*
Spell **Sagittarius** and the related word **Sagittarian** with one **g** and a double **t**.

sailor *noun*
Remember that **sailor** ends with **-or**.

salary *noun*
Remember that **salary** ends with **-ary**.

> **RULE:** Make the plural of words that end in a consonant plus **-y** by changing the **-y** to **-ies**: salaries.

saleable *adjective*
Saleable can also be spelled **salable**, without the middle **e**, although this is far less common.

salmon *noun*
Remember that **salmon** is spelled with an **l** in the middle.
TIP: salmon were leaping upstream.

salvo *noun*
The plural of **salvo** can be spelled **salvos** or **salvoes**, although **salvos** is more common.

samosa *noun*
Remember that **samosa** begins with **sam-**.

sandwich *noun and verb*
Remember that **sandwich** is spelled with a **d** after the **n**; the ending is **-ich** (it is named after the 4th Earl of *Sandwich*).

sapphire *noun*
Spell **sapphire** with a double **p**, followed by an **h**.

sari *noun*
Sari (a Hindi word) can also be spelled **saree**, with a double **e**: both are correct.

satchel *noun*
Remember that **satchel** has a **t** in the middle.

satellite *noun*
Spell **satellite** with two single **t**'s and a double **l**.

sauté *adjective and verb* (sautés, sautéing, sautéed or sautéd)
Sauté is a French word and is usually spelled with an accent on the **e**, although **saute** is also correct.

saviour *noun*
Remember that **saviour** ends with **-iour** (the spelling **savior** is American).

savour *verb*
Remember that **savour** and the related word **savoury** are spelled with **-our** (the spellings **savor** and **savory** are American).

scallop *noun and verb*
Spell **scallop** with a double **l** and a single **p**.

Scandinavian *adjective and noun*
Remember that **Scandinavian** is spelled with **-din-** in the middle.

scarf *noun*
The plural of **scarf** can be spelled **scarves** or **scarfs**, although **scarves** is much more common.

scary *adjective*
Remember that **scary** ends with **-ry**.

scenario *noun* (plural scenarios)
Spell **scenario** with an **a** after the **n**.

sceptic *noun*
Remember that **sceptic** begins with **sc-** (the spelling **skeptic** is American).
! Do not confuse **sceptic** with **septic**. *See* **SEPTIC**.

sceptre *noun*
Remember that **sceptre** begins with **sc-** and that the ending is **-re** (the spelling **scepter** is American).

schnapps *noun*
Spell **schnapps** with **schn-** at the beginning, then a double **p**: it is a German word.

science *noun*
Spell **science** with **sci-** at the beginning.
RELATED WORDS: scientific *adjective*, scientist *noun*

scintillate *verb*
Spell **scintillate** with a double **l**.

scissors *plural noun*
Remember that **scissors** begins with **sc-** and has a double **s** in the middle.
TIP: **s**nipping and **c**utting with the **s**mall **s**harp **s**cissors.

scrumptious *adjective*
Remember that **scrumptious** is spelled with a **p** after the **m**.

sculptor *noun*
The ending of **sculptor** is spelled **-or**.

scurrilous *adjective*
Spell **scurrilous** with a double **r** and one **l**.

scythe *noun and verb*
Remember that **scythe** begins with **scy-** and has an **e** at the end.

sebaceous *adjective*
Remember that **sebaceous** ends with **-ceous**.

s

secede *verb*
Remember that **secede** ends with **-cede**. *See centre pages for other verbs that end in -cede or -ceed.*

secretary *noun* (plural secretaries)
Spell **secretary** with an **e** after the **r**; the ending is **-ary**.

secrete *verb*
Remember that **secrete** ends with **-ete**.

sedentary *adjective*
Remember that **sedentary** ends with **-ary**.

segue *verb and noun*
Remember that **segue** (an Italian word) is spelled very differently from the way in which it is said: it ends with **-gue**.

seismic *adjective*
The beginning of **seismic** is spelled **sei-**.

seize *verb*
Remember that **seize** and the related word **seizure** are spelled with the **e** before the **i**: they do not follow the rule of **i** before **e** except after **c**.

selector *noun*
The ending of **selector** is spelled **-or**.

semaphore *noun and verb*
Spell **semaphore** with **-ph-** in the middle.

senator *noun*
The ending of **senator** is spelled **-or**.

sensible *adjective*
Remember that the ending of **sensible** is spelled **-ible**.

sensor *noun*
The ending of **sensor** is spelled **-or**.

sentence *noun and verb*
The ending of **sentence** is spelled **-ence**.

separate *verb and adjective*
Remember that **separate** is spelled with **-par-** in the middle.
TIP: the rock split into two se**par**ate **par**ts.
RELATED WORD: separation *noun*

septic *adjective*
❗ Do not confuse **septic** with **sceptic**. **Septic** means 'infected with bacteria' (*septic wounds*), whereas **sceptic** means 'a person who questions accepted beliefs or statements' (*numerous sceptics poured scorn on his claim*).

sequoia *noun*
The ending of **sequoia** is spelled **-oia** (the tree was named after *Sequoya*, a Cherokee Indian).

serenade *noun and verb*
Remember that **serenade** is spelled with **-ren-** in the middle.

sergeant *noun*
The beginning of **sergeant** is spelled **ser-**; the ending is **-geant**.

serial *adjective and noun*
❗ Do not confuse **serial** with **cereal**. *See* **CEREAL**.

serrated *adjective*
Spell **serrated** with a double **r**.

serviceable *adjective*

RULE: Keep the final **-e** when adding **-able** to *service* to make sure that **serviceable** is pronounced with a soft *-ce-* sound: servi**ce**able.

sesame *noun*
Spell **sesame** with a single **s** in the middle; the ending is **-me**.

several *adjective*
Remember that **several** is spelled with -ver- in the middle.
TIP: there are several versions of the game.

Shakespearean *adjective*
Shakespearean can also be spelled **Shakespearian**: both are correct.

shallot *noun*
Spell **shallot** with a double **l**.

sheaf *noun*

> **RULE:** Change the -f to -ves to make the plurals of nouns that end in a consonant or a single vowel plus -f or -fe: sheaves.

shear *verb*
The different forms of this verb are: shears, shearing, sheared; the past participle is shorn or sheared.
❗ Do not confuse **shear** with **sheer**. **Shear** means 'cut the wool off a sheep'. As a verb, **sheer** means 'change course quickly' (*the road sheered off into the darkness*); **sheer** is also an adjective chiefly meaning 'nothing but; absolute' (*the sheer joy of skydiving*).

sheikh *noun*
Sheikh (an Arabic word) can also be spelled **sheik**, **shaykh**, or **shaikh**, although **sheikh** is the most common.

shelf *noun*

> **RULE:** Change the -f to -ves to make the plurals of nouns that end in a consonant or a single vowel plus -f or -fe: shelves.

shepherd *noun and verb*
The ending of **shepherd** is spelled -herd.

sherbet *noun*
Remember that there is only one **r** in **sherbet**: the ending is -et.

TIP: can you eat two sherbet sweets at once?

sheriff *noun*
Spell **sheriff** with one **r** and a double **f**.

shibboleth *noun*
Spell **shibboleth** with a double **b**: it is a Hebrew word.

shield *noun and verb*

> **RULE:** i before e, except after c (as in *thief*).

shovel *noun and verb*

> **RULE:** Double the **l** when adding endings which begin with a vowel to words which end in a vowel plus **l** (as in *travel*): shovels, shovelling, shovelled.

shriek *noun and verb*

> **RULE:** i before e, except after c (as in *thief*).

shrivel *verb*

> **RULE:** Double the **l** when adding endings which begin with a vowel to words which end in a vowel plus **l** (as in *travel*): shrivels, shrivelling, shrivelled.

siege *noun*

> **RULE:** i before e except after c (as in *thief*).

sieve *noun and verb*
Remember that **sieve** is spelled with sie- at the beginning.

sight *verb and noun*
❗ Do not confuse **sight** with **site**. **Sight** means 'the ability to see' (*he lost his sight in an accident*), whereas **site** means 'a place where something is located or happens' (*the site of a famous temple*).

S

signal ▶ sleigh

signal *noun* and *verb*

RULE: Double the **l** when adding endings which begin with a vowel to words which end in a vowel plus **l** (as in *travel*): signals, signalling, signalled.

signatory *noun* (plural signatories)
The ending of **signatory** should be spelled **-ory**.

signature *noun*
Remember that **signature** is spelled with **-nat-** in the middle.

signet *noun*
❗ Do not confuse **signet** with **cygnet**. *See* **CYGNET**.

significant *adjective*
The ending of **significant** is spelled **-ant**.
RELATED WORD: significance *noun*

silhouette *noun* and *verb*
Remember that **silhouette** is spelled with an **h** after the **l**.
TIP: a silhouette of a large head.

silicon *noun*
❗ Do not confuse **silicon** with **silicone**. **Silicon** is a chemical element used in electronic circuits and microchips, whereas **silicone** is the material used in cosmetic implants.

similar *adjective*
Remember that the ending of **similar** is spelled **-lar**.

simile *noun*
The ending of **simile** is spelled **-ile**.

simultaneous *adjective*
Remember that **simultaneous** ends with **-eous**.

sincere *adjective*
The ending of **sincere** should be spelled **-cere**.
RELATED WORD: sincerely *adverb*

singe *verb* and *noun*

RULE: Keep the final **-e** when adding **-ing** so as to tell the difference between **singeing** and **singing** (the present participle of *sing*): singes, singeing, singed.

-sion
See centre pages for words ending in -sion and -tion.

siphon *noun* and *verb*
Siphon can also be spelled **syphon**, with a **y**: both are correct.

site *noun* and *verb*
❗ Do not confuse **site** with **sight**. *See* **SIGHT**.

sizeable *adjective*
Sizeable can also be spelled **sizable**, without the **e**: both are correct.

skein *noun*
Spell **skein** with the **e** before **i**.

skeleton *noun*
Remember that **skeleton** begins with **skele-**.

ski *noun* and *verb* (skis, skiing, skied)

RULE: Make the plural of **ski** in the usual way, by adding **-s**: skis.

RELATED WORD: skier *noun*

skilful *adjective*
Remember that **skilful** is spelled with one **l** in the middle (the spelling **skillful** is American).

RULE: If a word ends in a double **l**, drop the last **l** when adding endings which begin with a consonant (here, **skill** plus **-ful**): skilful.

sleigh *noun*
Spell **sleigh** with **-ei-** after the **l**; the ending is **-gh**.

sleight of hand *noun*
Remember that **sleight** is spelled with -**ei**- after the **l**; the ending is -**ght**.

sluice *noun and verb*
Remember that **sluice** has an **i** after the **u**.

smidgen *noun*
Smidgen can also be spelled **smidgeon**, with an **o** before the **n**: both are correct, although **smidgen** is far more common.

smoky *adjective*
Spell **smoky** with -**ky** at the end.

smooth *adjective and verb*
The verb **smooth** is sometimes spelled **smoothe**, with an **e** at the end.

smorgasbord *noun*
Remember that the ending of **smorgasbord** (a Swedish word) is spelled -**bord**.

smoulder *verb*
Spell **smoulder** with a **u** in the middle (the spelling **smolder** is American).

snivel *verb*

> **RULE:** Double the **l** when adding endings which begin with a vowel to words which end in a vowel plus **l** (as in *travel*): snivels, snivelling, snivelled.

snorkel *noun and verb*

> **RULE:** Double the **l** when adding endings which begin with a vowel to words which end in a vowel plus **l** (as in *travel*): snorkels, snorkelling, snorkelled.

sobriquet *noun*
Sobriquet can also be spelled **soubriquet**, with a **u** after the **o**: it is a French word.

software *noun*
Remember that the ending of **software** is spelled -**ware**, as are similar words to do with computer software (such as *groupware*).

soirée *noun*
Soirée is a French word and it is usually spelled with an accent on the first **e**, although **soiree** is also correct.

solemn *adjective*
Remember that **solemn** ends with -**mn**.
RELATED WORD: solemnity *noun*

solicit *verb*
Spell **solicit** with a single **l**.

solicitor *noun*
Remember that **solicitor** is spelled with a single **l**; the ending is -**or**.

sombre *adjective*
Remember that **sombre** ends with -**bre** (the spelling **somber** is American).

somersault *noun and verb*
Spell **somersault** with **somer**- at the beginning; the ending is -**sault**.

somnolent *adjective*
Remember that **somnolent** is spelled with -**ent** at the end.

sonorous *adjective*
Spell **sonorous** with -**nor**- in the middle.

sorbet *noun*
Remember that **sorbet** ends in -**et**: the **t** is not spoken because it is a French word.

soufflé *noun*
Soufflé is a French word and is usually spelled with an accent on the **e**, although **souffle** is also correct.

S

soulless *adjective*
Spell **soulless** with a double **l** (it is made up of the word **soul** and the ending **-less**).
TIP: his soulless and lonely life.

soupçon *noun*
Soupçon is a French word, and should be spelled with an accent (called a cedilla) below the **c**.

sovereign *noun and adjective*
Remember that the ending of **sovereign** is spelled **-eign**.
RELATED WORD: sovereignty *noun*

spaghetti *plural noun*
Spaghetti (an Italian word) is spelled with an **h** after the **g**; the ending is **-tti**.

spatial *adjective*
Remember that the ending of **spatial** is spelled **-tial**.

speciality *noun* (plural **specialities**)
The normal spelling is **speciality**; the spelling **specialty**, without the **i** before the **t**, is found in American English and some medical uses.

species *noun*
The plural of **species** is the same as the singular. Remember that the ending is **-ies**.

specimen *noun*
Remember that the ending of **specimen** is spelled **-men**.

spectator *noun*
The ending of **spectator** should be spelled **-or**.

spectre *noun*
Remember that **spectre** ends with **-re** (the spelling **specter** is American).

spectrum *noun*
Make the plural of **spectrum** by changing the **-um** ending to **-a** (as in Latin): **spectra**.

sphinx *noun*
Remember that **sphinx** is spelled with **sph-** at the beginning.

spicy *adjective*
> **RULE:** If a word ends in a consonant plus **-y**, change the **-y** to an **-i** before adding any ending (unless the ending already begins with an **-i**): spicier, spiciest.

spinach *noun*
Remember that the ending of **spinach** is spelled **-ach**.

spiral *adjective and verb*
> **RULE:** Double the **l** when adding endings which begin with a vowel to words which end in a vowel plus **l** (as in *travel*): spirals, spiralling, spiralled.

splendour *noun*
Remember that **splendour** ends with **-our** (the spelling **splendor** is American).

sponsor *noun and verb*
The ending of **sponsor** is spelled **-or**.

spontaneous *adjective*
Remember that **spontaneous** ends with **-neous**.

sprightly *adjective*
Sprightly can also be spelled **spritely**: both are correct, although **sprightly** is far more common.

spurt *verb and noun*
Remember that **spurt** is spelled with a **u** in the middle.

spy *noun and verb*
> **RULE:** If a word ends in a consonant plus **-y** (as in *defy*), change the **-y** to an **-i** before adding any ending (unless the

S

squalor *noun*
Remember that the ending of **squalor** is spelled -or.
RELATED WORD: squalid *adjective*

squirrel *noun and verb*

> **RULE:** Double the **l** when adding endings which begin with a vowel to words which end in a vowel plus **l** (as in *travel*): squirrels, squirrelling, squirrelled.

squirt *verb and noun*
Remember that **squirt** is spelled with -**ui**- in the middle.

staccato *adverb and adjective*
Spell **staccato** with a double **c**.

stadium *noun*
The plural of **stadium** can be spelled either **stadiums** or **stadia** (like the original Latin).

stake *verb and noun*
❗ Do not confuse **stake** with **steak**. **Stake** mainly means 'gamble money or something valuable' (*he staked everything he'd got and lost*), 'a strong post used to support plants', or 'something gambled' (*playing dice for high stakes*), whereas **steak** means 'a thick slice of beef' (*steak and chips*).

stalactite *noun*
❗ Do not confuse **stalactite** with **stalagmite**. A **stalactite** hangs from the roof of a cave, whereas a **stalagmite** rises up from a cave's floor.
TIP: stalactites hang from the **c**eiling; stalagmites start from the **g**round.

stampede *verb and noun*
Remember that **stampede** ends with -**ede**.

stationary *adjective*
❗ Do not confuse **stationary** with **stationery**. **Stationary** means 'not moving or changing' (*the lorry hit a line of stationary vehicles*), whereas **stationery** means 'paper and other writing materials'.
TIP: the c**a**r was station**a**ry; station**e**ry is pap**e**r.

statuesque *adjective*
The ending of **statuesque** is spelled -**esque**.

staunch *verb*
Remember that **staunch** is spelled with -**au**- in the middle (the spelling **stanch** is American).

steady *adjective, verb, and noun*

> **RULE:** If a word ends in a consonant plus -**y**, change the -**y** to an -**i** before adding any ending (unless the ending already begins with an -**i**): steadier, steadiest.
>
> **RELATED WORDS:** steadily *adverb*, steadiness *noun*

steak *noun*
❗ Do not confuse **steak** with **stake**. See **STAKE**.

stellar *adjective*
Remember that the ending of **stellar** is spelled -**ar**.

stencil *noun and verb*

> **RULE:** Double the **l** when adding endings which begin with a vowel to words which end in a vowel plus **l** (as in *travel*): stencils, stencilling, stencilled.

stile *noun*
❗ Do not confuse **stile** with **style**. **Stile** means 'steps set into a fence or wall for people to climb over', whereas **style** means 'a way of doing something' (*different styles of management*).

S

stiletto *noun* (plural **stilettos**)
Spell **stiletto** (an Italian word) with a single **l** and a double **t**.

stimulant *noun*
The ending of **stimulant** is spelled **-ant**.

stimulus *noun*
Make the plural of **stimulus** by changing the **-us** ending to **-i** (as in Latin): **stimuli**.

stirrup *noun*
Spell **stirrup** with a double **r**.

stomach *noun and verb*
Remember that **stomach** ends with **-ach**.

> **RULE:** If a noun ends in **-ch** and is pronounced *-k*, make the plural by adding an **-s**: **stomachs**.

stop *verb and noun*

> **RULE:** If a one-syllable word ends with a single vowel plus a consonant, double the last letter when adding **-ing** or **-ed**: **stops**, **stopping**, **stopped**.

storage *noun*
Remember that **storage** ends with **-age**.

story *noun*
! Do not confuse **story** with **storey**. **Story** means 'an account told to people to entertain them' (*an adventure story*), whereas **storey** means 'a floor of a building' (*a three-storey house*). In American English, the spelling **story** is used for both senses.

straight *adjective*
! Do not confuse **straight** with **strait**. **Straight** means 'without a curve or bend' (*a long, straight road*), whereas **strait** means 'a narrow passage of water' (*the Straits of Gibraltar*) or 'trouble or

difficulty' (*many hospitals are in dire straits*).

straitjacket *noun*
Straitjacket can also be spelled **straightjacket**: both are correct.

strait-laced *adjective*
Strait-laced can also be spelled **straight-laced**: both are correct.

strategy *noun* (plural **strategies**)
Remember that the beginning of **strategy** and the related word **strategic** should be spelled **stra-**.

stratum *noun*
The plural of **stratum** is **strata** (as in the original Latin).

strength *noun*
Remember that **strength** is spelled with a **g** before the **-th**.
TIP: a man of **g**reat stren**g**th.

strident *adjective*
Remember that **strident** ends with **-ent**.

stucco *noun*
Spell **stucco** with a double **c**: it is an Italian word.

study *verb and noun*

> **RULE:** If a word ends in a consonant plus **-y** (as in *defy*), change the **-y** to an **-i** before adding any ending (unless the ending already begins with an **-i**): **studies**, **studying**, **studied**.

stupefy *verb*
Remember that **stupefy** ends with **-efy**. *See centre pages for words ending in -ify and -efy.*

stupor *noun*
The ending of **stupor** is spelled **-or**.

style *verb and noun*
! Do not confuse **style** with **stile**. *See* **STILE**.

S

suave *adjective*
Remember that **suave** is spelled with a **u** before the **a**.
TIP: a s**u**ave and **u**rbane **a**ristocrat.

subjugate *verb*
Remember that **subjugate** is spelled with a **j** in the middle.

submersible *adjective and noun*
The ending of **submersible** is spelled **-ible**.

submit *verb*

> **RULE:** If a verb ends with a single vowel plus a consonant, and the stress is at the end of the word (as in *refer*), double the last letter when adding **-ing** or **-ed**: submits, submitting, submitted.

subsequent *adjective*
The ending of **subsequent** is spelled **-ent**.

subsidiary *adjective and noun*
(plural subsidiaries)
Remember that **subsidiary** is spelled with **-iary** at the end.

subsistence *noun and adjective*
Remember that **subsistence** ends with **-ence**.

subterranean *adjective*
Subterranean is spelled with a double **r**; the ending is **-ean**.

subtle *adjective*
Remember that **subtle** and the related word **subtlety** have a silent **b** before the **t**.
TIP: the wine is a su**bt**le **b**lend of **t**wo grapes.

succeed *verb*
The ending of **succeed** is spelled **-ceed**. *See centre pages for other verbs that end in -cede or -ceed.*

success *noun*
Spell **success** and the related word **successful** with a double **c** and a double **s**.
RELATED WORD: successor *noun*

succession *noun*
Remember that **succession** and the related word **successive** are spelled with a double **c** and a double **s**.

succinct *adjective*
Spell **succinct** with a double **c** in the middle, then a single **c** before the final **t**.

succour *noun and verb*
Remember that **succour** ends with **-our** (the spelling **succor** is American).

succulent *adjective and noun*
Spell **succulent** with a double **c**; the ending is **-ent**.

succumb *verb*
Remember that **succumb** is spelled with a double **c**; there is a silent **b** at the end.

sue *verb*

> **RULE:** Drop the final silent **-e** when adding **-ing** or **-ed**: sues, suing, sued.

suede *noun*
Remember that **suede** is spelled with **-ue-** after the **s**.

sufferance *noun*
Remember that **sufferance** has an **e** in the middle; the ending is **-ance**.

sufficient *adjective*
Spell **sufficient** with a double **f**; the ending is **-cient**.

suffrage *noun*
Remember that **suffrage** begins with **suffr-**
RELATED WORD: suffragette *noun*

s

suggest *verb*
Spell **suggest** and the related words **suggestion** and **suggestive** with a double **g**.
RELATED WORD: suggestible *adjective*

suitor *noun*
The ending of **suitor** is spelled **-or**.

sulphur *noun*
Sulphur, and the words related to it such as *sulphate* and *sulphuric*, are spelled with an **f** in American English and also by scientists: *sulfur*, *sulfate*, *sulfuric*, etc.

summary *adjective and noun*
(plural **summaries**)
Spell **summary** with a double **m**; the ending is **-ary**.

sundae *noun*
Remember that **sundae** ends with **-ae**.

supercilious *adjective*
Remember that **supercilious** is spelled with **-cil-** in the middle.

superficial *adjective*
The ending of **superficial** is spelled **-cial**.

superintendent *noun*
The ending of **superintendent** is spelled **-ent**.

supersede *verb*
The ending of **supersede** is spelled **-sede**; it is the only verb with this ending. *See centre pages for verbs that end in* **-cede** *or* **-ceed**.

superstitious *adjective*
Remember that **superstitious** ends with **-itious**.

supervise *verb*
Unlike most verbs ending in **-ise**, **supervise** cannot be spelled with an **-ize** ending. *See centre pages for other verbs that always end in* **-ise**.
RELATED WORD: supervisor *noun*

supplementary *adjective*
Remember that **supplementary** ends with **-ary**.

supply *noun and verb*

> **RULE:** If a word ends in a consonant plus **-y** (as in *defy*), change the **-y** to an **-i** before adding any ending (unless the ending already begins with an **-i**): supplies, supplying, supplied.

RELATED WORD: supplier *noun*

support *verb*
Remember that **support** and the related word **supporter** are spelled with a double **p**.

suppose *verb*
Spell **suppose** with a double **p**.

suppress *verb*
Spell **suppress** with a double **p** and a double **s**.

surfeit *noun*
Remember that **surfeit** is spelled with the **e** before the **i**.

surgeon *noun*
The ending of **surgeon** is spelled **-geon**.

surmise *verb and noun*
Unlike most verbs ending in **-ise**, **surmise** cannot be spelled with an **-ize** ending. *See centre pages for other verbs that always end in* **-ise**.

surplus *noun*
Remember that **surplus** ends with a single **s**.

> **RULE:** Add **-es** to make the plural of words which end in **-s**: surpluses.

surprise *verb and noun*
Remember that **surprise** has an **r** before and after the **p**. Unlike most verbs ending in **-ise**, it cannot be spelled with an **-ize** ending. *See centre pages for other verbs that always end in* **-ise**.

surreal *adjective*
Spell **surreal** with a double **r**.

surrender *verb and noun*
Surrender is spelled with a double **r**.

surveillance *noun*
Remember that **surveillance** is spelled **-ei-** in the middle, then a double **l**.

surveyor *noun*
The ending of **surveyor** is **-or**.

survivor *noun*
Spell **survivor** with **-or** at the end.

susceptible *adjective*
Remember that **susceptible** has a **c** after the second **s**; the ending is **-ible**.

suspense *noun*
Remember that **suspense** ends with **-ense**.

suspicious *adjective*
The ending of **suspicious** is spelled **-cious**.
RELATED WORD: suspicion *noun*

sustenance *noun*
Spell **sustenance** with **-ance** at the end.

swap *noun and verb* (swaps, swapping, swapped)
Swap can also be spelled **swop**, with an **o**: both are correct.

swat *verb and noun*
! Do not confuse **swat** with **swot**. **Swat** means 'hit something with a flat object' (*he swatted some flies buzzing around him*), whereas **swot**

means 'study hard' (*kids swotting for GCSEs*) or 'a person who studies hard'.

swivel *verb*

> **RULE:** Double the **l** when adding endings which begin with a vowel to words which end in a vowel plus **l** (as in *travel*): swivels, swivelling, swivelled.

swot *verb and noun*
! Do not confuse **swot** with **swat**. *See* **SWAT**.

sycophant *noun*
Remember that **sycophant** begins with **syco-** and has **-ph-** in the middle.

syllable *noun*
Spell **syllable** with a double **l** in the middle; the ending is **-able**.

syllabus *noun*
The plural can be spelled either **syllabi** (like the original Latin) or **syllabuses**.

symmetry *noun*
Remember that **symmetry** begins with **sy-** and has a double **m** in the middle.

sympathy *noun* (plural sympathies)
Remember that **sympathy** and the related word **sympathize** (or **sympathise**) begin with **sym-**.

symphony *noun* (plural symphonies)
Spell **symphony** with **sym-** at the beginning, then **-ph-**.

symposium *noun*
The plural of **symposium** can be spelled either **symposia** (as in Latin) or **symposiums**.

s

synagogue *noun*
Spell **synagogue** with **-gogue** at the end

synonym *noun*
Remember that **synonym** ends with **-nym**.
RELATED WORD: synonymous *adjective*

synopsis *noun*

> **RULE:** Make the plural of **synopsis** by changing the **-is** ending to **-es**: synopses.

synthesis *noun*

> **RULE:** Make the plural of **synthesis** by changing the **-is** ending to **-es**: syntheses.

syringe *noun and verb*
Remember that **syringe** begins with **sy-**.

syrup *noun*
The beginning of **syrup** is spelled **sy-** (the spelling **sirop** is American).

tableau *noun*
The plural of **tableau** can be spelled either **tableaux** (like the original French) or **tableaus**.

taco *noun*

> **RULE:** Make the plural of **taco** in the usual way, by adding **-s**: tacos.

taffeta *noun*
Remember that **taffeta** is spelled with a double **f**; the ending is **-eta**.

tagine *noun*
Tagine can also be spelled **tajine**: it is an Arabic word.

tagliatelle *plural noun*
Remember that **tagliatelle** ends with **-elle**: it is an Italian word.

tail *noun and verb*
! Do not confuse **tail** with **tale**. **Tail** means 'the rear or end part of an animal or thing' (*the dog wagged its tail*), whereas **tale** means 'a story' (*a fairy tale*).

tambourine *noun*
Spell **tambourine** with **-our-** in the middle.

tangible *adjective*
The ending of **tangible** is spelled **-ible**.

tango *noun and verb* (tangoes, tangoing, tangoed)

> **RULE:** Make the plural of **tango** in the usual way, by adding **-s**: tangos.

target *noun and verb*

> **RULE:** Do not double the final consonant when adding endings which begin with a vowel to a word which ends in a vowel plus a consonant, if the stress is not at the end of the word: targets, targeting, targeted.

tariff *noun*
Spell **tariff** with one **r** and a double **f**.

tarragon *noun*
Spell **tarragon** with a double **r**.

tattoo *noun and verb* (tattoos, tattooing, tattooed)
Remember that **tattoo** is spelled with a double **t** and a double **o**.

> **RULE:** Make the plural of the noun in the usual way, by adding **-s**: tattoos.

taxi *verb* (taxies, taxiing or taxying, taxied) and *noun*
Taxiing can also be spelled **taxying**, with a **y**.

> **RULE:** Make the plural of the noun in the usual way, by adding **-s**: taxis.

-tch
See centre pages for words ending in **-tch** *and* **-ch**.

team *noun and verb*
! Do not confuse **team** with **teem**. **Team** means 'a group of people

working or playing together' or 'come together as a team to achieve something' (*the two governors teamed up against their opponent*), whereas **teem** means 'be full of something' (*the seas teemed with fish*).

technician *noun*
The ending of **technician** is spelled **-cian**.

technique *noun*
Remember that **technique** ends with **-que**.

teem *verb*
❗ Do not confuse **teem** with **team**. *See* **TEAM**.

televise *verb*
Unlike most verbs ending in **-ise**, **televise** cannot be spelled with an **-ize** ending. *See centre pages for other verbs that always end in* **-ise**.

temperament *noun*
Remember that **temperament** is spelled with **-era-** in the middle. **TIP:** a man of mod**era**te temp**era**ment.

temperance *noun*
The ending of **temperance** is spelled **-ance**.

temperature *noun*
Spell **temperature** with **-era-** in the middle.

temporal *adjective*
Remember that **temporal** is spelled with **-or-** in the middle.

temporary *adjective*
The ending of **temporary** is spelled **-orary**.

tendency *noun* (plural **tendencies**)
Remember that **tendency** ends with **-ency**.

tenor *noun*
Spell **tenor** with a single **n**: the ending is **-or**.

tenuous *adjective*
Remember that **tenuous** ends with **-uous**.

terminus *noun*
The plural of **terminus** can be spelled either **termini** (like the original Latin) or **terminuses**.

terracotta *noun*
Spell **terracotta** with a double **r** and a double **t**: it is from an Italian phrase meaning 'baked earth'.

terrazzo *noun*
Spell **terrazzo** (an Italian word) with a double **r** and a double **z**.

terrestrial *adjective*
Remember that **terrestrial** is spelled with a double **r** in the middle.

terrible *adjective*
Spell **terrible** with a double **r**; the ending is **-ible**.

terrify *verb* (**terrifies, terrifying, terrified**)
Remember that the ending of **terrify** is spelled **-ify**. *See centre pages for words ending in* **-ify** *and* **-efy**.

territory *noun* (plural **territories**)
Spell **territory** with a double **r** in the middle; the ending is **-ory**.

testament *noun*
Spell **testament** with **-ta-** in the middle.

tête-à-tête *noun*
Tête-à-tête is a French phrase (meaning 'head-to-head'), and it is usually spelled with the accents shown here.

theatre *noun*
Remember that **theatre** ends with -tre (the spelling **theater** is American).
RELATED WORD: theatrical *adjective*

their *adjective*
❗ Do not confuse **their** with **there** or **they're**. *See* **THERE**.
Remember that **their** is spelled with the **e** before the **i**.

theirs *pronoun*
Although **theirs** is a possessive pronoun (one that is used to show belonging), it should not be spelled with an apostrophe before the **s**. *See centre pages for more information about apostrophes.*

therapeutic *adjective*
Remember that **therapeutic** is spelled with -**eu**- in the middle.

there *adverb*
❗ Do not confuse **there** with **their** or **they're**. **There** means 'in, at, or to that place' (*it took an hour to get there*); **their** means 'belonging to them' (*I went to their house*); **they're** is short for **they are** (*they're a good team*).

thesaurus *noun*
Spell **thesaurus** with -**au**- in the middle. The plural can be spelled either **thesauruses** or **thesauri** (like the original Latin).

thesis *noun*

> **RULE:** Make the plural by changing the -**is** ending to -**es**: theses.

they're
❗ Do not confuse **they're** with **there** or **their**. *See* **THERE**.

thief *noun*

> **RULE:** **i** before **e** except after **c**.

The plural of **thief** is **thieves**.

thorough *adjective*
❗ Do not confuse **thorough** with **through**. **Thorough** means 'done with great care and completeness' (*officers made a thorough examination of the wreckage*), whereas **through** means 'in one side and out the other' (*she stepped boldly through the door*).

though *conjunction and adverb*
Spell **though** with -**ough** at the end.

thought *noun*
The ending of **thought** is spelled -**ought**.

threshold *noun*
Remember that **threshold** is spelled with a single **h**.

throes *plural noun*
❗ Do not confuse **throes** with **throws**. **Throes** means 'great pain or difficulty' (*a country in the throes of a civil war*), whereas **throws** is the present tense of the verb 'to throw' (*he throws his stuff into the car*) or the plural of the noun **throw** (*three throws of the dice*).

thrombosis *noun*

> **RULE:** Make the plural of **thrombosis** by changing the -**is** ending to -**es**: thromboses.

through *prepostion*
❗ Do not confuse **through** with **thorough**. *See* **THOROUGH**.

tidy *adjective and verb* (tidies, tidying, tidied)

> **RULE:** If a word ends in a consonant plus -**y**, change the -**y** to an -**i** before adding any ending (unless the ending already begins with an -**i**): tidier, tidiest.

RELATED WORDS: tidily *adverb*, tidiness *noun*

tie verb and noun

> **RULE:** When a verb ends with **-ie**, change the **-ie** ending to **-y** when adding **-ing**: ties, tying, tied.

tikka noun
Spell **tikka** (a Punjabi word) with a double **k**.

timorous adjective
Remember that **timorous** is spelled with **-or-** in the middle.

tinge noun and verb (tinges, tingeing or tinging, tinged)
Tingeing can also be spelled **tinging**, without an **e**; both are correct.

-tion
See centre pages for words ending in -tion and -sion.

tiptoe verb (tiptoes, tiptoeing, tiptoed)
Keep the **e** in **tiptoeing**; it does not follow the usual rule that a final silent **e** is dropped when adding endings that begin with a vowel.

tiramisu noun
Spell **tiramisu** (an Italian word) with one **r** and one **m**: the ending is **-isu**.

titillate verb
Spell **titillate** with a double **l**.

titular adjective
Remember that **titular** ends with **-ar**.

to preposition
❗ Do not confuse **to** with **too** or **two**. **To** usually means 'in the direction of' (*the next train to London*); **too** means 'excessively' (*you're driving too fast*); **two** is the number between one and three.

tobacco noun
Spell **tobacco** with one **b** and a double **c**.
TIP: **b**reathing in to**b**acco smoke **c**auses **c**ancer.

toboggan noun
Remember that **toboggan** is spelled with one **b** and a double **g**.

toe noun and verb (toes, toeing, toed)
Keep the **e** in **toeing**; it does not follow the usual rule that a final silent **e** is dropped when adding endings that begin with a vowel.
❗ Do not confuse **toe** with **tow**. The correct phrase is **toe the line**, which originally meant 'stand with the tips of the toes exactly touching a line' (for instance, at the start of a race).

toffee noun
Spell **toffee** with a double **f** and a double **e**.

tofu noun
Spell **tofu** (a Chinese word) with **-fu** at the end.

tolerance noun
Remember that **tolerance** is spelled with a single **l**; the ending is **-ance**.
RELATED WORD: tolerant adjective

tomato noun
The plural of **tomato** is made by adding **-es**: tomatoes.

tomorrow adverb and noun
Spell **tomorrow** with a single **m** and a double **r**.
TIP: to**m**orrow **m**orning, **r**ise **r**efreshed.

tongue noun and verb

> **RULE:** Drop the final silent **-e** when adding **-ing** or **-ed**: tongues, tonguing, tongued.

t

too *adverb*
! Do not confuse **too** with **to** or **two**.
See **TO**.

tooth *noun*
The plural of **tooth** is **teeth**.

tornado *noun*
The plural of **tornado** can be spelled either **tornadoes** or **tornados**.

torpedo *noun and verb* (torpedoes, torpedoing, torpedoed)
The plural of **torpedo** is made by adding **-es**: **torpedoes**.

torpor *noun*
Remember that **torpor** ends with **-or**.

torrent *noun*
Spell **torrent** with a double **r**: the ending is **-ent**.

tortellini *noun*
Spell **tortellini** with a double **l** and a single **n**: it is an Italian word.

tortilla *noun*
Remember that **tortilla** (a Spanish word) is spelled with a double **l**.

total *noun and verb*

> **RULE:** Double the **l** when adding endings which begin with a vowel to words which end in a vowel plus **l** (as in *travel*): **totals, totalling, totalled**.

> **RELATED WORD:** **totally** *adverb*

toupee *noun*
Toupee is a French word and it can also be spelled **toupée**, with an accent on the first **e**.

tournament *noun*
Remember that there is an **a** in the middle of **tournament**.

tourniquet *noun*
The ending of **tourniquet** is spelled **-quet**: the **t** is not spoken because it is a French word.

tow *verb and noun*
! Do not confuse **tow** with **toe**. *See* **TOE**.

towel *noun and verb*

> **RULE:** Double the **l** when adding endings which begin with a vowel to words which end in a vowel plus **l** (as in *travel*): **towels, towelling, towelled**.

tractor *noun*
The ending of **tractor** is spelled **-or**.

traffic *noun and verb*

> **RULE:** If a verb ends in **-ic** (as in *picnic*), add a **k** after the **c** when adding **-ed**, **-ing**, and **-er**: **traffics, trafficking, trafficked**.

> **RELATED WORD:** **trafficker** *noun*

tragedy *noun* (plural tragedies)
Spell **tragedy** with **-g-** in the middle.
TIP: tra**g**edy began in ancient Greece.

traipse *verb and noun*
Remember that **traipse** is spelled with **-ai-** in the middle.

traitor *noun*
Remember that **traitor** ends with **-or**.

tranquil *adjective*
Remember that **tranquil** ends with a single **l**.

tranquillity *noun*

> **RULE:** Double the **l** when adding endings which begin with a vowel to words which end in a vowel plus **l** (here, *tranquil*): **tranquillity**.

t

tranquillize, tranquillise *verb*
Remember that **tranquillize** is spelled with a double **l** (the spelling **tranquilize** is American).

transcend *verb*
Spell **transcend** and the related word **transcendent** with **-sc-** in the middle.

transfer *verb and noun*

> **RULE:** If a verb ends with a single vowel plus a consonant, and the stress is at the end of the word (as in *refer*), double the last letter when adding **-ing** or **-ed**: transfers, transferring, transferred.

transient *adjective and noun*
Remember that **transient** ends with **-ent**.

transitory *adjective*
Remember that **transitory** ends with **-ory**.

translator *noun*
Spell **translator** with **-or** at the end.

translucent *adjective*
Remember that **translucent** ends with **-cent**.

transmit *verb*

> **RULE:** If a verb ends with a single vowel plus a consonant, and the stress is at the end of the word (as in *refer*), double the last letter when adding endings which begin with a vowel: transmits, transmitting, transmitted.

> **RELATED WORD:** transmitter *noun*

transparent *adjective*
The ending of **transparent** is spelled **-ent**.
RELATED WORD: transparency *noun*

trattoria *noun*
Remember that **trattoria** (an Italian word) is spelled with a double **t** in the middle and a single **r**.

travel *noun and verb*

> **RULE:** Double the **l** when adding endings which begin with a vowel to words which end in a vowel plus **l**: travels, travelling, travelled.

> **RELATED WORD:** traveller *noun*

treacherous *adjective*
Remember that **treacherous** and the related word **treachery** begin with **trea-**.

trek *noun and verb*

> **RULE:** If a one-syllable word ends with a single vowel plus a consonant (as in *stop*), double the last letter when adding **-ing** or **-ed**: treks, trekking, trekked.

trellis *noun*
Remember that **trellis** is spelled with a double **l**.

tremor *noun*
The ending of **tremor** is spelled **-or**.

trenchant *adjective*
Remember that **trenchant** ends with **-ant**.

trespass *verb*
Spell **trespass** with a single **s** in the middle and a double **s** at the end.

trial *noun and verb*

> **RULE:** Double the **l** when adding endings which begin with a vowel to words which end in a vowel plus **l** (as in *travel*): trials, trialling, trialled.

triangular *adjective*
The ending of **triangular** is spelled **-ar**.

tributary *noun* (plural **tributaries**)
The ending of **tributary** is spelled **-ary**.

triceps *noun*
The plural of **triceps** is the same as the singular: **triceps**.

triumph *noun*
Remember that **triumph** ends with **-mph**.
RELATED WORD: triumphant *adjective*

trousseau *noun*
The plural of **trousseau** can be spelled either **trousseaux** (as in the original French) or **trousseaus**.

truculent *adjective*
The ending of **truculent** is spelled **-ent**.

truism *noun*
There is no **e** in **truism**. *See* **TRULY**.

truly *adverb*

> **RULE:** **Truly** is formed from **true** (minus the silent **e**) plus the ending **-ly**.

truncheon *noun*
Remember that **truncheon** ends with **-eon**.

try *verb and noun*

> **RULE:** If a word ends in a consonant plus **-y** (as in *defy*), change the **-y** to an **-i** before adding any ending (unless the ending already begins with an **-i**): tries, trying, tried.

> **RELATED WORD:** trier *noun*

tsar *noun*
Tsar can also be spelled **czar**, especially when it is used to mean 'a person with authority or power in a particular area' (*he's the nation's next drug czar*).

T-shirt *noun*
T-shirt can also be spelled **tee shirt**: both are correct.

tubular *adjective*
The ending of **tubular** is spelled **-ar**.

tumour *noun*
The ending of **tumour** is **-our** (the spelling **tumor** is American).

tunnel *noun and verb*
Spell **tunnel** with a double **n** and a single **l**.

> **RULE:** Double the **l** when adding endings which begin with a vowel to words which end in a vowel plus **l** (as in *travel*): tunnels, tunnelling, tunnelled.

turbulent *adjective*
The ending of **turbulent** is spelled **-ent**.

turmeric *noun*
Remember that there is an **r** before the **m** in **turmeric**.
TIP: **r**ice and **m**eat flavoured with turmeric.

turnstile *noun*
The ending of **turnstile** is spelled **-ile**.

turquoise *noun*
Remember that **turquoise** ends with **-quoise**.

turret *noun*
Spell **turret** with a double **r** and a single **t** at the end.

tutor *noun and verb*
Remember that **tutor** ends with **-or**.

t

tuxedo *noun*
The plural of **tuxedo** can be spelled either **tuxedoes** or **tuxedos**.

twelfth *number*
Remember that **twelfth** has an **f** in the middle.
TIP: go to the twelfth **f**loor of the building.

two *number*
! Do not confuse the number **two** with **to** or **too**. *See* **TO**.

tyranny *noun*
Spell **tyranny** and the related word **tyrannical** with one **r** and a double **n**.

tyrant *noun*
Remember that **tyrant** ends with **-ant**.

tyre *noun*
Spell **tyre** with a **y** (the spelling **tire** is American).

t

ubiquitous *adjective*
Remember that **ubiquitous** is spelled with **-quit-** in the middle.

ugly *adjective*

> **RULE:** If a word ends in a consonant plus **-y**, change the **-y** to an **-i** before adding any ending (unless the ending already begins with an **-i**): **uglier, ugliest**.
>
> **RELATED WORD:** ugliness *noun*

ultimatum *noun*
The plural of **ultimatum** is usually spelled **ultimatums**, although **ultimata** (as in the original Latin) is also correct.

umbrella *noun*
Remember that **umbrella** is spelled **umbr-** at the beginning.

unattached *adjective*
Spell **unattached** with a double **t**, then **-ach-**.

unbelievable *adjective*

> **RULE:** **i** before **e**, except after **c** (as in *receive*).

unbiased *adjective*
Spell **unbiased** with a single **s**.

unbridgeable *adjective*
Remember that **unbridgeable** is spelled with an **e** in the middle, as well as one at the end.
TIP: an unbridgeable gap between each edge.

uncomplimentary *adjective*
Spell **uncomplimentary** with -li- in the middle.

underprivileged *adjective*
The ending of **underprivileged** is spelled **-leged**.

underrate *verb*
Remember that **underrate** is spelled with a double **r** (it is made up of the words **under-** and **rate**).

undeterred *adjective*
Spell **undeterred** with one **t** and a double **r**.

unembarrassed *adjective*
Remember that **unembarrassed** is spelled with a double **r** and a double **s**.

unequalled *adjective*
Spell **unequalled** with a double **l** (the spelling **unequaled** is American).

unfavourable *adjective*
Spell **unfavourable** with -ou- in the middle (the spelling **unfavorable** is American).

unfocused *adjective*
Unfocused can also be spelled **unfocussed**, with a double **s**; both are correct.

unforeseen *adjective*
Remember that **unforeseen** is spelled with **-fore-** in the middle.
RELATED WORD: unforeseeable *adjective*

unforgettable *adjective*
Spell **unforgettable** with a double **t**; the ending is **-able**.

unforgivable *adjective*
Remember that **unforgivable** ends with **-able**.

unfortunately *adverb*
Spell **unfortunately** with **-ately** at the end (it is made up of the adjective **unfortunate** plus the ending **-ly**).

unintelligible
Spell **unintelligible** with a double **l** in the middle; the ending is **-ible**.

uninterested *adjective*
! Do not confuse **uninterested** with **disinterested**. *See* **DISINTERESTED**.

uninterrupted *adjective*
Remember that **uninterrupted** is spelled with a double **r**.

unlicensed *adjective*
The ending of **unlicensed** is spelled **-sed**.

unmistakable *adjective*
Unmistakable can also be spelled **unmistakeable**, with an **e** after the **k**: both are correct.

unnatural *adjective*
Remember that **unnatural** is spelled with a double **n** (it is made up of the beginning **un-** plus the adjective **natural**).

unnecessary *adjective*
Spell **unnecessary** with a double **n**, a single **c**, and a double **s**.

unprejudiced *adjective*
Remember that **unprejudiced** is spelled with **-prej-** in the middle.

unprofessional *adjective*
Spell **unprofessional** with a single **f** and a double **s**.

unravel *verb*

> **RULE:** Double the **l** when adding endings which begin with a vowel to words which end in a vowel plus **l** (as in *travel*): **unravels**, **unravelling**, **unravelled**.

unrivalled *adjective*
Unrivalled is spelled with a double **l** (the spelling **unrivaled** is American).

unsavoury *adjective*
The ending of **unsavoury** is **-oury** (the spelling **unsavory** is American).

unshakeable *adjective*
Unshakeable can also be spelled **unshakable**, without the **e** in the middle: both are correct.

unskilful *adjective*
Remember that **unskilful** is spelled with one **l** in the middle and one at the end (the spelling **unskillful** is American).

> **RULE:** If a word ends in a double **l**, drop the last **l** when adding endings which begin with a consonant (here, **skill** plus **-ful**): **unskilful**.

unsuccessful *adjective*
Spell **unsuccessful** with a double **c** and a double **s**.

until *preposition and conjunction*
Spell **until** with a single **l**.

unwarranted *adjective*
Spell **unwarranted** with a double **r**, then an **a**.

unwieldy *adjective*

> **RULE:** **i** before **e** except after **c** (as in *thief*).

urge *verb and noun*

> **RULE:** Drop the final silent **-e** when adding **-ing** or **-ed**: **urges**, **urging**, **urged**.

usable *adjective*
Usable can also be spelled **useable**, with an **e** in the middle: both are correct.

usage *noun*

> **RULE:** **Usage** is formed from **use** (minus the silent **e**) plus the ending **-age**.

usual *adjective*
Usual is spelled with a **u** after the **s**, as well as one before it.
RELATED WORD: **usually** *adverb*

utensil *noun*
Remember that **utensil** ends with **-sil**.

utilize, utilise *verb*
Spell **utilize** and the related word **utilization** with a single **l**.

utterance *noun*
The ending of **utterance** is spelled **-ance**.

u

vaccinate *verb*
Remember that **vaccinate** and the related word **vaccination** are spelled with a double **c**.

vacillate *verb*
Spell **vacillate** and the related word **vacillation** with one **c** and a double **l**.

vacuum *noun and verb*
Remember that **vacuum** is spelled with a double **u**. The plural can be spelled either **vacuums** or **vacua** (as in the original Latin).

vagrant *noun and adjective*
The ending of **vagrant** is spelled **-ant**.

vain *adjective*
❗ Do not confuse **vain** with **vane** or **vein**. **Vain** means 'having a very high opinion of yourself' (*a vain woman with a touch of snobbery*) or 'without success or a result' (*a vain attempt to tidy up*); **vein** means 'a tube that carries blood around the body' or 'a particular style or quality' (*he continued in a more serious vein*); **vane** means 'a broad blade forming part of a windmill, propeller, or turbine'.

valance *noun*
The ending of **valance** is spelled **-ance**.

valiant *adjective*
Spell **valiant** with **-ant** at the end.

valorous *adjective*

> **RULE:** If a word ends in **-our** (in this case *valour*), change **-our** to **-or** before adding **-ous** and some other endings: **valorous**.

valour *noun*
The ending of **valour** is **-our** (the spelling **valor** is American).

valuable *adjective*
Remember that **valuable** ends with **-able**.

vane *noun*
❗ Do not confuse **vane** with **vain** or **vein**. *See* **VAIN**.

vanilla *noun*
Spell **vanilla** with one **n** and a double **l**.

vapour *noun*
Spell **vapour** with **-our** at the end (the spelling **vapor** is American).

variegated *adjective*
Remember that **variegated** and the related word **variegation** are spelled with an **e** in the middle.
TIP: plant variegated **e**vergreens for winter colour.

variety *noun* (plural **varieties**)
Spell **variety** with **-ie-** in the middle.

various *adjective*
The ending of **various** is **-ious**.

vary *verb*

> **RULE:** If a word ends in a consonant plus **-y** (as in *defy*), change the **-y** to an **-i** before adding any ending (unless the ending already begins with an **-i**): varies, varying, varied.

RELATED WORDS: variable *adjective*, variant *noun*

vector *noun*
The ending of **vector** is spelled **-or**.

vegetable *noun*
Vegetable is spelled with an **e** after the **g**, as well one as before it.

vegetarian *noun and adjective*
Remember that the beginning of **vegetarian** is spelled **vege-**; the ending is **-arian**.

vehement *adjective*
The ending of **vehement** is **-ent**.
RELATED WORD: vehemence *noun*

vehicle *noun*
Spell **vehicle** with **-icle** at the end.

vein *noun*
! Do not confuse **vein** with **vain** or **vane**. *See* **VAIN**.

venal *adjective*
! Do not confuse **venal** with **venial**. **Venal** means 'open to bribery' (*venal politicians*), whereas **venial** is used, especially in Christianity, to mean 'a sin or offence that is excusable or pardonable'.

vendetta *noun*
Spell **vendetta** with a double **t**: it is an Italian word.

vengeance *noun*
Remember that **vengeance** is spelled with **-ea-** after the **g**.

ventilator *noun*
The ending of **ventilator** is spelled **-or**.

veranda *noun*
Veranda can also be spelled **verandah**, with an **h**; both are correct.

verdant *adjective*
Remember that **verdant** ends with **-ant**.

verify *verb*

> **RULE:** If a word ends in a consonant plus **-y** (as in *defy*), change the **-y** to an **-i** before adding any ending (unless the ending already begins with an **-i**): verifies, verifying, verified.

RELATED WORD: verifiable *adjective*

verisimilitude *noun*
Spell **verisimilitude** with **veri-** at the beginning.

vermicelli *plural noun*
Spell **vermicelli** with a single **c** but a double **l**: it is an Italian word.

vermilion *noun*
Remember that there is only one **l** in **vermilion**.

verruca *noun*
Spell **verruca** with a double **r** but a single **c**. The plural can be spelled either **verrucas** or **verrucae** (as in the original Latin).

versatile *adjective*
Remember that **versatile** and the related word **versatility** are spelled with **-sat-** in the middle.
TIP: a ver**sat**ile **sat**in blouse.

vertebra *noun*
The plural of **vertebra** is **vertebrae** (as in the original Latin).

vertebrate *noun and adjective*
Spell **vertebrate** with **-teb-** in the middle.

v

vertex *noun*
The plural of **vertex** can be spelled either **vertices** (as in the original Latin) or **vertexes**.

vessel *noun*
Spell **vessel** with a double **s**; the ending is **-el**.

veterinary *adjective*
Remember that **veterinary** is spelled with **-er-** after the **t**; the ending is **-ary**.

veto *noun and verb* (vetoes, vetoing, vetoed)
The plural of the noun is made by adding **-es**: **vetoes**.

vibrant *adjective*
The ending of **vibrant** is **-ant**.

vibrator *noun*
Spell **vibrator** with **-or** at the end.

vice *noun*
When used to mean 'a tool used to hold something in place', **vice** is spelled **vise** in American English.

vichyssoise *noun*
Spell **vichyssoise** with a double **s**; the soup is named after the French town of *Vichy*.

vicious *adjective*
Remember that the beginning of **vicious** is spelled **vici-**.

victor *noun*
The ending of **victor** is spelled **-or**.

video *noun and verb*

> **RULE:** Make the plural of the noun in the usual way, by adding **-s**: video**s**.

The verb forms are: videoes, videoing, videoed.

Viennese *adjective and noun*
Remember that **Viennese** is spelled with a double **n**.

vigilant *adjective*
The ending of **vigilant** is spelled **-ant**.

vigorous *adjective*

> **RULE:** If a word ends in **-our** (in this case *vigour*), change **-our** to **-or** before adding **-ous** and some other endings: **vigorous**.

vigour *noun*
Remember that **vigour** ends with **-our** (the spelling **vigor** is American).

vilify *verb*
Remember that **vilify** and the related word **vilification** are spelled with a single **l**.

villain *noun*
Spell **villain** with a double **l**; the ending is **-ain**.

vinaigrette *noun*
Vinaigrette is spelled with **-ai-** after the **n**: it is a French word.

vinegar *noun*
Spell **vinegar** with an **e** after the **n**; the ending is **-ar**.

violence *noun*
Remember that **violence** ends with **-ence**.
RELATED WORD: violent *adjective*

virago *noun*
The plural of **virago** can be spelled either **viragos** or **viragoes**.

virtuoso *noun*
The plural of **virtuoso** can be spelled **virtuosi** (as in the original Italian) or **virtuosos**.

virulent *adjective*
Remember that **virulent** ends with **-ent**.
RELATED WORD: virulence *noun*

V

virus *noun*

> **RULE:** Add **-es** to make the plural of words ending in **-s**: **viruses**.

vis-à-vis *preposition*
Vis-à-vis is usually spelled with an accent on the **a** (as in the original French).

visceral *adjective*
Remember that **visceral** is spelled with **-sc-** in the middle.

visible *adjective*
The ending of **visible** is spelled **-ible**.

visionary *adjective and noun* (plural **visionaries**)
Remember that **visionary** ends with **-ary**.

visit *verb and noun*

> **RULE:** Do not double the final consonant when adding endings which begin with a vowel to a word which ends in a vowel plus a consonant, if the stress is not at the end of the word (as in *target*): visits, visiting, visited.

> **RELATED WORD:** visitor *noun*

visor *noun*
Visor can also be spelled **vizor**, although **visor** is much more common.

vitamin *noun*
The ending of **vitamin** is spelled **-min**.

TIP: vitamins and minerals are essential to health.

vivacious *adjective*
Spell **vivacious** and the related word **vivacity** with a **c** in the middle.

vocabulary *noun*
Remember that **vocabulary** ends with **-ary**.

volcano *noun*
The plural of **volcano** can be spelled either **volcanoes** or **volcanos**.

voluntary *adjective*
Remember that **voluntary** ends with **-tary**.

vortex *noun*
The plural of **vortex** can be spelled either **vortexes** or **vortices** (as in the original Latin).

vowel *noun*
The ending of **vowel** is spelled **-el**.

voyeur *noun*
The ending of **voyeur** (a French word) is spelled **-eur**.

vulgar *adjective*
The ending of **vulgar** is spelled **-ar**.

vulnerable *adjective*
Remember that **vulnerable** is spelled with an **l** before the **n**.

v

wagon *noun*
Wagon can also be spelled **waggon**, with a double **g**; both are correct.

waist *noun*
❗ Do not confuse **waist** with **waste**. *See* **WASTE**.

waive *verb*
❗ Do not confuse **waive** with **wave**. **Waive** means 'give up a claim or right' (*he will waive all rights to the money*), whereas **wave** means 'move to and fro' (*the flag waved in the wind*) or 'a ridge of water on the sea'.

waiver *noun*
❗ Do not confuse **waiver** with **waver**. *See* **WAVER**.

wallaby *noun* (plural wallabies)
Remember that **wallaby** is spelled with a double **l**.

walnut *noun*
There is only one **l** in **walnut**.

warrant *noun and verb*
Spell **warrant** with a double **r**; the ending is **-ant**.
RELATED WORD: warranty *noun*

warrior *noun*
The ending of **warrior** is spelled **-ior**.

waste *verb and noun*
❗ Do not confuse **waste** with **waist**. **Waste** means 'use more of something than is necessary or useful' (*we can't afford to waste electricity*), whereas **waist** means

'the part of a person's body between the ribs and the hips' (*he put his arm around her waist*).

wave *verb and noun*
❗ Do not confuse **wave** with **waive**. *See* **WAIVE**.

waver *verb*
❗ Do not confuse **waiver** with **waver**. **Waver** means 'move in a quivering way' or 'be undecided' (*she never wavered from her intention*), whereas a **waiver** is a legal document recording that a right or claim has been given up.

weapon *noun*
Remember that **weapon** and the related word **weaponry** are spelled with an **a** after the **e**.

weary *adjective and verb* (wearies, wearying, wearied)

> **RULE:** If a word ends in a consonant plus **-y**, change the **-y** to an **-i** before adding any ending (unless the ending already begins with an **-i**): wearier, weariest.

RELATED WORDS: wearily *adverb*, weariness *noun*

weather *noun and verb*
❗ Do not confuse **weather** with **wether** or **whether**. **Weather** means 'conditions in the atmosphere such as temperature, rain, etc.' (*if the weather's good we'll go for a walk*); a **wether** is a castrated male sheep; **whether** means 'if', or is used to show doubt

or a choice (*she wasn't sure whether to be flattered or outraged*).

Wednesday *noun*
Remember that **Wednesday** is spelled with a **d** before the **n**, although it is not heard when you say the word.

weight *noun and verb*
Spell **weight** with the **e** before the **i**, then **-ght**.

weir *noun*
Weir is spelled with the **e** before the **i**: it does not follow the usual rule of **i** before **e** except after **c**.

weird *adjective*
Remember that **weird** is spelled with the **e** before the **i**: it does not follow the usual rule of **i** before **e** except after **c**.
TIP: a **wei**rd, **ee**rie, inhuman sound.

wet *adjective and verb*
! Do not confuse **wet** with **whet**. See **WHET**.

wether *noun*
! Do not confuse **wether** with **weather** or **whether**. See **WEATHER**.

whereas *conjunction*
Spell **whereas** with an **e** before the **a**; it is made up of the words **where** and **as**.

wherever *adverb*
Remember that **wherever** is spelled with a single **e** after the first **r**.

wherewithal *noun*
Spell **wherewithal** with a single **l** at the end.

whet *verb*
! Do not confuse **whet** with **wet**. **Whet** means 'excite someone's interest or appetite' (*this recipe should whet your appetite*), whereas **wet** means 'covered or saturated

with liquid' (*I slipped on the wet rock*) or 'make someone or something wet' (*he wet his lips, then spoke*).

whether *conjunction*
! Do not confuse **whether** with **weather** or **wether**. See **WEATHER**.

whimsy *noun*
Spell **whimsy** and the related word **whimsical** with **wh-** at the beginning.

whinge *verb* (**whinges**, **whingeing** or **whinging**, **whinged**)
Whingeing can also be spelled **whinging**, without an **e**; both are correct.

whisky *noun*
When referring to the alcoholic spirit from Scotland, use the spelling **whisky** (plural **whiskies**). **Whiskey**, with an **e** (plural **whiskeys**), is the spelling used in Ireland and America.

wholly *adverb*
The ending of **wholly** is spelled **-lly**.

who's
! Do not confuse **who's** with **whose**. **Who's** is short for **who is** (*he has a son who's a doctor*) or **who has** (*who's done the reading?*), whereas **whose** means 'belonging to which person' (*whose coat is this?*) or 'of whom or which' (*he's a man whose opinion I respect*).

width *noun*
Remember that **width** is spelled with **-dth** at the end.

wield *verb*
RULE: i before **e** except after **c** (as in *thief*).

wife *noun*
RULE: Change the **-fe** to **-ves** to make the plurals of nouns that end

w

in a consonant or a single vowel plus **-f** or **-fe**: *wives*.

wiles *plural noun*
Remember that **wiles** and the related word **wily** begin with **wi-**.

wilful *adjective*
Remember that **wilful** is spelled with one **l** in the middle (the spelling **willful** is American).

RULE: If a word ends in a double **l**, drop the last **l** when adding endings which begin with a consonant (here, **will** plus **-ful**): **wilful**.

wintry *adjective*
Remember that, although it is related to *winter*, **wintry** ends with **-try**.

withdrawal *noun*
Spell **withdrawal** with **-wal** at the end (it is made up of the word **withdraw** and the ending **-al**).

withhold *verb* (withholds, withholding, withheld)
Remember that **withhold** is spelled with a double **h** (it is made up of the words **with** and **hold**)

wolf *noun*

RULE: Change the **-f** to **-ves** to make the plurals of nouns that end in a consonant or a single vowel plus **-f** or **-fe**: *wolves*.

wondrous *adjective*
Remember that **wondrous** is spelled with **-dr-** in the middle.

woollen *adjective*
Remember that **woollen** is spelled with a double **l** (the spelling **woolen** is American).

worry *noun* and *verb*

RULE: If a word ends in a consonant plus **-y** (as in *defy*), change the **-y** to an **-i** before adding any ending (unless the ending already begins with an **-i**): *worries*, *worrying*, *worried*.

RELATED WORDS: worrier *noun*, worrisome *adjective*

worship *noun* and *verb*
Worship is an exception to the rule that you only double the last letter when adding endings which begin with a vowel to a word ending in a vowel plus a consonant if the stress is at the *end* of the word. In this case, the stress is at the *beginning* of the word, but you should still double the **p**: worships, worshipping, worshipped.
RELATED WORD: worshipper *noun*

wrack *verb*
! Do not confuse **wrack** with **rack**. See **RACK**.

wrap *noun* and *verb* (wraps, wrapping, wrapped)
Remember that **wrap** is spelled with a **w** at the beginning, although it is not heard when you say the word. Other words that begin with **wr-** include *wrath*, *wreak*, *wreck*, *wrench*, *wrestle*, *wriggle*, *wrist*, *write*, and *wrong*.

wring *verb* (wrings, wringing, wrung)
! Do not confuse **wring** with **ring**. **Wring** means 'twist or squeeze something' (*I wanted to wring his neck*), whereas the verb **ring** mainly means 'surround someone or something' (*the courthouse was ringed with police*) or 'make a clear sound' (*a bell started to ring*).

W

wry *adjective*

The comparative and superlative (**-er** and **-est** forms) of **wry** can be spelled with a **y** or an **i**: wryer, wryest or wrier, wriest.

RELATED WORD: wryly *adverb*

Xx Yy Zz

xenophobia *noun*
Remember that **xenophobia** and the related word **xenophobic** begin with an **x**.

xylophone *noun*
The beginning of **xylophone** is spelled **xylo-**.

yacht *noun and verb*
Remember that the ending of **yacht** is spelled **-acht**.

yield *verb and noun*

> **RULE:** **i** before **e** except after **c** (as in *receive*).

> **TIP:** the study should y**ie**ld important **e**vidence.

yogurt *noun*
Yogurt can also be spelled **yoghurt** or **yoghourt**: all three are correct.

yoke *noun and verb*
! Do not confuse **yoke** with **yolk**. **Yoke** means 'a piece of wood fastened over the necks of two animals' or 'bring people or things into a close relationship' (*Hong Kong's dollar has been yoked to America's*), whereas **yolk** means 'the yellow part of an egg'.

your
! Do not confuse **your** with **you're**. **Your** means 'belonging to you' (*let me talk to your daughter*), whereas **you're** is short for **you are** (*you're a good cook*).

yours *pronoun*
Although **yours** is a possessive pronoun (one that is used to show belonging), it should not be spelled with an apostrophe before the **s**. *See centre pages for more information about apostrophes.*

-yse
See centre pages for verbs ending in **-yse***,* **-ise***, and* **-ize***.*

zabaglione *noun*
Spell **zabaglione** (an Italian word) with a **g** in the middle and **-ione** at the end.

zeitgeist *noun*
Remember that **zeitgeist** (a German word) is spelled with **-ei-** after the **z** and again after the **g**.

zero *number and verb* (zeroes, zeroing, zeroed)

> **RULE:** Make the plural of **zero** in the usual way, by adding **-s**: zeros.

zigzag *noun and verb*

> **RULE:** If a verb ends with a single vowel plus a consonant, and the stress is at the end of the word (as in *refer*), double the last letter when adding **-ing** or **-ed**: zigzags, zigzagging, zigzagged.

zoo *noun*

> **RULE:** Make the plural of **zoo** in the usual way, by adding **-s**: zoos.

> **RELATED WORDS:** zoologist *noun*, zoology *noun*